7
SECRETS TO PURPOSEFUL LIVING

Unlocking Your Path to Happiness and Fulfillment

NITA FLEMING

Chennai • Bangalore

CLEVER FOX PUBLISHING
Chennai, India

Published by CLEVER FOX PUBLISHING 2024
Copyright © Nita Fleming 2024

All Rights Reserved.
ISBN: 978-93-56487-78-9

This book has been published with all reasonable efforts taken to make the material error-free after the consent of the author. No part of this book shall be used, reproduced in any manner whatsoever without written permission from the author, except in the case of brief quotations embodied in critical articles and reviews.

The Author of this book is solely responsible and liable for its content including but not limited to the views, representations, descriptions, statements, information, opinions and references ["Content"]. The Content of this book shall not constitute or be construed or deemed to reflect the opinion or expression of the Publisher or Editor. Neither the Publisher nor Editor endorse or approve the Content of this book or guarantee the reliability, accuracy or completeness of the Content published herein and do not make any representations or warranties of any kind, express or implied, including but not limited to the implied warranties of merchantability, fitness for a particular purpose. The Publisher and Editor shall not be liable whatsoever for any errors, omissions, whether such errors or omissions result from negligence, accident, or any other cause or claims for loss or damages of any kind, including without limitation, indirect or consequential loss or damage arising out of use, inability to use, or about the reliability, accuracy or sufficiency of the information contained in this book.

Dedication

"To the brave souls who dare to confront the uncomfortable truths of life, who question the status quo, and who refuse to settle for mediocrity, this book is dedicated to you. May its pages challenge, inspire, and occasionally entertain you on your journey towards a more honest and fulfilling existence. And to my family and friends who have endured my endless musings and existential crises, thank you for your patience and support. Thanks to my incredible coach, Jatin, without you, this would not have been possible.

EPIGRAPH

"*In* the journey of purpose, the heart finds its map, the soul its compass, and life its true rhythm, echoing with the timeless truth: 'The answers you seek never come when the mind is busy. They come when the mind is still.'"

ACKNOWLEDGMENTS

Alright, folks, here we are at the obligatory "thank you" section.

As I sit down to express my gratitude, I find myself humbled by the journey that led to this book. It's a testament to the power of purpose and the unwavering support of those around me. So, let's give credit where it's due.

First, big thanks to my Jesus and the Holy Spirit. Your teachings on purpose and fulfillment have been the backbone of this whole operation, and I can't thank you enough for that divine inspiration.

To you readers stumbling upon these pages, whether you're here on purpose or just along for the ride, thanks for giving this book a shot. Hope you find something worthwhile in my ramblings.

And a special shoutout to my rockstar Coach, Jatin. Your unwavering support and constant encouragement have been instrumental in silencing my inner critic and inspiring me to sit down and pen these words.

To my ever-supportive family—My Mom, Marjorie, My Husband Terence, my daughter Candy, and my Son Dennis you've been the wind beneath my wings. Your belief in me when I doubted myself? Priceless. It means the world to me. You are my pillar of strength, and I am forever grateful for your presence in my life.

Oh, and I can't forget my furry pals Tyson and Twinkle. More than just pets, you've been my sanity in the chaos, my cuddly confidants when the writing got tough.

And to my Spiritual Directors, Rev Sistes and all my friends, colleagues, and media mates who've had my back, you're the Most Valuable Players.

Lastly, a nod to the universe for throwing me those curveballs. They weren't always fun, but they sure kept things interesting. Here's to embracing the chaos and finding purpose in the mess.

Alright, it's enough. Let's get back to living purposefully, shall we?"

Much Love,

Nita Fleming

INTRODUCTION:

Welcome to "7 Secrets to Purposeful Living: Unlocking Your Path to Happiness and Fulfilment."

Greetings, readers! Welcome aboard the rollercoaster ride of existence, where every twist and turn promises a chance for self-discovery, purpose, and that elusive thing we call fulfillment. Fasten up your set belt, because we're about to dive headfirst into the deep end of life's pool, armed with nothing but curiosity and a thirst for meaning.

Imagine this: You find yourself perched on the edge of a cliff, the wind whispering in your ears, the abyss below calling out to you. That's life, my friend—wild, unpredictable, and oh-so-tempting to take a leap into the unknown. But fear not, for it's in these moments of uncertainty that the real magic happens.

So, buckle up, and let's take a deep dive into the depths of our own existence. We're gearing up to shake up the status quo, toss conformity out the window, and unearth the keys to sculpting a life that's more than just going through the motions—it's a grand symphony of joy and purpose.

But hey, before we get too serious, let me share a little story from my own life. You're at the grocery store, faced with the monumental decision of crunchy or creamy peanut butter. Sounds trivial, right? But hold up. It's a decision of epic proportions, right up there with choosing a career path or finding your soulmate. And in that seemingly ordinary moment, it hits you like a ton of bricks—life's a buffet of choices, each one shaping our journey in ways we never expected. So, whether it's peanut butter preferences or existential crises, remember: every choice counts.

So, my readers, get ready to laugh and cry as we navigate the maze of existence together. Because if life's a wild ride, then consider this book your ticket to the front-row seat of the greatest show on Earth. Let's do this!

A Brief Overview

All right folks, get ready for a sneak peek at what's in store as we kick off this life-changing journey together!

Prepare to set sail on a voyage unlike any other—a quest for purposeful living. In the upcoming chapters, we'll unravel the mysteries of happiness and fulfillment, guiding you towards a life illuminated by clarity, purpose, and unwavering intention.

The Path Ahead

Get ready to strap on your helmets because diving headfirst into a whirlwind of insights, exercises, and real-world wisdom is designed to equip you for life's unpredictable twists and turns. From discovering your authentic purpose to conquering challenges and finding inspiration in the most unexpected corners, think of this as your personal guidebook to empowerment.

Key Themes and Topics

Throughout our expedition, we'll explore the core themes of self-discovery, resilience, and authenticity. Each chapter promises a treasure trove of invaluable insights and practical tools to fuel your journey towards purposeful living.

Practical Guidance

But wait, there's more! We're not just here to philosophize—we're here to roll up our sleeves and get down to business. Inside, you'll discover many hands-on activities and down-to-earth techniques to breathe life into these concepts and kickstart your transformation. Whether you're facing a monumental life decision or simply seeking more gusto in your daily grind, consider us your partners in purpose.

Embracing Imperfection

Please repeat after me: perfection is overrated. Embrace the beautiful chaos of life's journey, celebrating each stumble and triumph along the way. Remember, perfection is overrated. Embrace life's messy, imperfect journey, and celebrate every step forward, no matter how small. Each chapter will give you fresh perspectives and resilient strategies to navigate life's obstacles with grace and gusto.

Conclusion

So, are you ready to dive in and uncover the secrets to purposeful living? Together, let's embark on this exhilarating quest towards a life bursting with clarity, passion, and unbridled fulfillment. The journey begins now—let's make every moment count!

The path awaits—let's explore it hand in hand!

PROLOGUE

*A*midst the chaos of existence, there echoes a timeless wisdom, whispered from the ages: "Fear not, for I am with you." In these pages, we'll navigate the depths of purposeful living, uncovering the mysteries that lie beneath the surface of our daily grind. So, buckle up, dear reader, for the adventure of a lifetime awaits.

CONTENTS

Epigraph .... *iv*
Acknowledgments .... *v*
Introduction .... *vii*
Prologue .... *xi*

Chapter 1. Unveiling Life's Purpose: A Journey Of Clarity 1

Chapter 2. Discovering Identity: Unveiling Your Role In The World 36

Chapter 3. Taking Charge: Directing Your Life's Course 61

Chapter 4. Navigating Challenges: Overcoming Obstacles On Your Path 88

Chapter 5. Fulfillment Unleashed: Balancing Passion And Reality 121

Chapter 6. Breaking Norms: Redefining Fulfillment On Your Own Terms 146

Chapter 7. Money Matters: Navigating Financial Wellness On Your Path To Purposeful Living 175

Author Biography *204*
Epilogue: Embracing The Journey Beyond *205*
Afterword *207*

CHAPTER 1

UNVEILING LIFE'S PURPOSE: A JOURNEY OF CLARITY

*H*ave you ever caught yourself staring into life's big questions, wondering why you're here on earth? Yeah, you're not alone. Join the club. Buckle up for a wild journey through this thing we call life as we pitch into some mind-blowing secrets that'll leave you reeling.

Imagine you're sitting alone, contemplating the stars in the night sky. In that moment of solitude, a nagging question arises: "What am I truly meant to do with my life?" It's a question that has plagued humanity for centuries, yet its answer remains elusive. Sounds familiar?

Let's cut through the noise and get real. Life's purpose isn't some abstract concept reserved for philosophers and mystics. It's a tangible force that drives us forward, shaping our decisions and actions. But here's the kicker: clarity is the key to unlocking this force.

Why should you care about finding clarity in your life's purpose? Well, clarity gives meaning to our existence. It guides us through the ups and downs, providing direction and fulfillment.

Ever notice how we humans tend to overcomplicate things? We'll explore some of the absurdities of our quest for purpose and poke fun at our existential dilemmas. After all, a good laugh can be just as enlightening as deep introspection.

What if the pursuit of clarity isn't about finding definitive answers but embracing life's uncertainty? We'll challenge the notion that clarity is a destination and instead view it as a continuous journey of self-discovery.

Enough theory; let's get practical. I'll share simple exercises to kickstart your journey towards clarity. From journal prompts to mindfulness practices, you'll have a toolkit of strategies to navigate the murky waters of purpose.

What's Next?

Ready to take the plunge? In the next chapter, we'll explore the concept of clarity more profoundly and explore practical methods for uncovering your life's purpose.

But for now, I'll leave you with this question:

What insights have you gained about your life's purpose?

1.1. Understanding the Concept of Life's Purpose

Have you ever pondered the age-old question: "What's the meaning of life?" Well, we're about to dive into some deep, logical waters.

Let me tell you about my friend Alex. For years, Alex stumbled through life like a sleepwalker in a carnival funhouse—lost, disoriented, and occasionally bumping into walls. Sound familiar?

Our mission here is crystal clear: strip away the layers of societal garbage and uncover the raw, unfiltered truth about what lights your fire. It's about getting real, getting honest, and getting down to the nitty-gritty of your soul.

Let's face it, and let's get real, folks. Wandering around like a lost puppy in a packed mall is not the vibe we're going for here. Figuring out your purpose isn't just some fluffy self-help idea—it's like having a GPS in the chaos of life.

Believe it or not, people have been wrestling with the whole "meaning of life" gig for ages. Some turn to religion, others to philosophy, whatever floats your boat.

Picture this: Sarah, a young woman in her mid-twenties, sits at her desk, staring out the window in unease. Despite her successes and accomplishments, she can't shake the feeling that something is missing. Sound familiar?

Ever notice how humans can spend hours debating the meaning of life over a lukewarm cup of coffee? We're trying to solve a Rubik's Cube with one hand tied behind our backs. At least we've got caffeine to keep us company.

Imagine a group of philosophers locked in a heated debate over the purpose of existence while the rest are just trying to figure out how to unclog a toilet. Life's funny like that—full of big questions and even bigger messes.

Here's a thought: what if life's purpose isn't some grand, cosmic plan written in the stars but a Choose Your Adventure book waiting for you to fill in the blanks? It's about embracing the uncertainty and crafting your own narrative.

Ready to roll up your sleeves and get to work? Get ready to dig deep and discover what makes you tick. Take a moment to reflect on your journey. What questions or doubts have been keeping you up at night? What small step can you take today to bring you closer to uncovering your purpose?

Reflective Question: What's one thing you've always wanted to pursue but have been too afraid to chase? It's time to grab the bull by the horns and take that first step towards living life on your own terms and conditions—though conditions apply.

1.2. The Benefits of Seeking Clarity in Life

Hey, did you ever feel like you were stumbling around in the dark, desperately searching for a light switch? Trust me, you're not the only one. In this section, we will highlight why clarity is crucial for navigating the murky waters of life.

Picture this: You're driving down a foggy road with zero visibility. Every turn feels like a blind gamble, and the destination seems more elusive than ever. Sound familiar? That's the feeling of wandering through life without clarity.

Meet John, a high-powered executive who seems to have it all—a corner office, a six-figure salary, and all the trappings of success. Yet, beneath the polished exterior lies a sense of restlessness and discontent. He's come to realize that material wealth alone doesn't guarantee fulfillment.

Now, let's get real for a moment. Why do we need clarity, anyway? Well, imagine trying to assemble a puzzle without the picture on the box. It's frustrating, confusing, and ultimately futile. Clarity is our guiding light, illuminating the path ahead and helping us make sense of the chaos.

But here's the kicker: clarity isn't just about knowing what you want; it's also about understanding what you don't want. It's about shedding light on the shadows of uncertainty and embracing the freedom to choose your own direction.

Now, I won't sugarcoat it. Let's cut to the chase—seeking clarity isn't a cakewalk. It's messy and uncomfortable, forcing us to confront our demons, stare down the abyss of the unknown, and question everything we thought we knew. But here's the kicker: it's worth it. Beyond that fog of uncertainty lies the crystal-clear vision and rock-solid confidence to chase your dreams like a boss.

So, how do people find clarity amidst the chaos of life? Well, there's no one-size-fits-all answer. Some turn to meditation, journaling, or long walks in nature. Others seek guidance from mentors, therapists, or trusted friends. And some stumble upon clarity in the most unexpected places—a chance encounter, a meaningful conversation, or a quiet moment of introspection.

Let's remember how humans can spend more time agonizing over which Netflix show to watch than contemplating our life's purpose. We're distracting ourselves from the big questions with trivialities. Sometimes, laughter is the best medicine for a soul weighed down by indecision.

Now, here's something to ponder: What if the search for clarity isn't about finding definitive answers but rather about embracing the uncertainty of life? It's about enjoying the process, surrendering to the unknown, and embracing the journey with open arms.

Reflective Question: Now, just take a moment to reflect on your own quest for clarity. What areas of your life feel foggy and uncertain? What steps can you take today to start shining a light on the path ahead?

1.3. The Challenges of Unveiling Life's Purpose

Imagine this: You're navigating through the complex journey of existence, but instead of breadcrumbs, you're leaving behind a trail of unanswered queries and bewilderment.

Welcome to the maze of uncertainty, where the signs of a lack of clarity abound.

Have you ever found yourself trapped in analysis paralysis, unable to make even the most straightforward decisions? Or you're constantly second-guessing yourself, wondering if you're on the right path or wandering aimlessly. These are just a few unmistakable signs that clarity has taken an extended vacation from your life.

Meet Emily, a recent college graduate navigating the choppy waters of post-graduation life. She finds herself caught in a whirlwind of uncertainty, unsure of which direction to take or where her true passions lie. Many of us can relate to this feeling—the sensation of being adrift in a sea of boundless possibilities.

Now, let's explore into how to spot these signs before they lead you astray. Pay heed to the persistent feeling in the pit of your stomach—the one that whispers, "Something's not right." It's your internal compass attempting to steer you back on course.

But here's the kicker: recognizing the signs is just the beginning. The real test lies in taking action to address them. So, how do you break free from this foggy funk and reclaim your clarity?

First off, let's tackle the elephant in the room—Fear – Do you fear making the wrong choice? fear of failure, fear of the unknown—like a dense fog that blocks our vision and paralyzes us from progressing. The Remedy? Courage. It's about acknowledging your fears without letting them control your decisions. Remember, courage isn't the absence of fear; it's the readiness to take action despite it.

Next up, let's tackle the perfectionist trap. You know, the one—constantly striving for an unattainable standard of perfection, where anything less feels like failure. It's time to embrace imperfection and permit yourself to make mistakes. After all, it's through our failures that we learn, grow, and ultimately find clarity.

And let's not forget about the comparison game—the unhealthy habit of measuring our worth against others' highlight reels. Spoiler alert: it's a losing battle. Instead of expending energy on comparisons, focus on cultivating self-awareness and defining success on your own terms.

Now, listen up, have you ever noticed how we humans can spend more time scrolling through Instagram than reflecting on our own lives? It's like we're addicted to the highlight reel, even though deep down, we know it's a carefully curated illusion. But hey, we're all guilty of occasionally falling into the comparison trap.

So, as we conclude this section, remember that clarity isn't a destination; it's a messy, unpredictable, and often downright frustrating journey. But amid the chaos, there's beauty—the opportunity to evolve, grow, and become the best version of ourselves.

Reflective Question: What fears hinder your pursuit of clarity, and what small steps can you take today to confront them head-on?

Action Steps:

1. Face Your Fears:
   - Recognize and list your fears, acknowledging their hold on you.
   - Confront them head-on by stepping out of your comfort zone or seeking support.
2. Be Kind to Yourself:
   - Practice self-compassion, treating yourself with empathy.
   - Define success on your terms and celebrate your journey, regardless of comparisons.
3. Manage Social Media Exposure:
   - Monitor social media impact, taking breaks or unfollowing negative triggers.
   - Remember, clarity takes time; focus on small, achievable steps each day.

1.4. Importance of Embarking on a Quest for Clarity

Welcome to a quest for clarity that promises to be as exhilarating as it is enlightening. In this section, we'll embark on this journey, which is both a luxury and a necessity for a fulfilling life.

Imagine yourself standing at the crossroads of possibility, surrounded by infinite paths stretching before you. Each one holds the potential for adventure, growth, and self-discovery. But here's the catch: you need clarity to navigate this maze of choices, stumbling over obstacles and veering off course.

Meet Tom, a middle-aged man who's spent decades climbing the corporate ladder, only to realize he's been climbing the wrong one. As he reflects on his life's journey, he comes to understand the importance of seeking clarity and purpose—it's the compass that guides us towards a life of meaning and fulfillment.

So, why is clarity so important anyway? Well, it's the compass that points you towards your true north—the guiding star that keeps you on track when life throws curveballs your way. Without it, you're adrift in a sea of indecision, tossed about by the whims of fate and circumstance.

But clarity is more than just a roadmap for navigating life's twists and turns. The key unlocks the door to your deepest desires, passions, and purpose. It's about stripping away the layers of noise and distraction to reveal the core of who you are and what you stand for.

Think about this: clarity is the difference between wandering aimlessly through a dense forest and confidently blazing your own trail. It's about knowing where you're going, why you're going there, and how to get there—a sense of purpose that infuses every step with meaning and intention.

Now, have you ever noticed how we can spend hours debating between two flavors of ice cream yet hesitate to explore the depths of our own aspirations? It's as if we're masters of distraction, expertly dodging profound questions with trivial pursuits. But amidst the lightheartedness, let's not forget the transformative power of enjoyment to illuminate our path and guide us to clarity.

So, here's the bottom line: embarking on a quest for clarity isn't a just pursuit—it's a non-negotiable step towards living a life of purpose, passion, and fulfillment. It's about embracing the unknown, trusting the process, and surrendering to the adventure that awaits.

As we conclude this section, take a moment to contemplate your personal journey. What motivated you to embark on this quest for understanding and clarity? Are there any fears or doubts that are limiting you from moving forward, and if so, how can you overcome them in order to confidently embrace the unknown?

Reflective Question: What's one small action you can take today to move closer to clarity and purpose in your life?

Action Steps:

Step 1: Carve Out Reflection Time

Allocate a few moments each day for introspection and reflection. Whether it's journaling, meditation, or simply quiet contemplation, create space to tune into your inner voice and aspirations.

Step 2: Define Your Why

Identify the driving force behind your quest for clarity. What values, aspirations, or dreams propel you forward? Understanding your motivations will provide clarity and direction as you navigate your journey.

Step 3: Embrace Curiosity

Approach the journey with a sense of curiosity and openness. Be willing to explore new perspectives, challenge assumptions, and embrace the unknown. Curiosity is the fuel that ignites the flames of discovery and growth.

Step 4: Take Inspired Action

Identify one small action you can take today to move closer to your clarity goals. Whether it's reaching out to a mentor, starting a new hobby, or setting boundaries to prioritize self-care, every step counts towards your journey of self-discovery.

Step 5: Cultivate Patience and Trust

Acknowledge that clarity is a gradual process that unfolds over time. Be patient with yourself and trust in the journey, knowing that each step forward brings you closer to living a life aligned with your purpose and passions.

1.5. Methods for Initiating Your Journey Towards Clarity

Welcome to the starting line of your clarity adventure—a journey promising profound growth and self-discovery. Here, we'll explore methods and strategies to ignite your journey and set you on the path to clarity.

Imagine yourself at the brink of possibility, a mix of excitement and nerves buzzing in your veins. It's a moment ripe with anticipation and uncertainty, yet deep down, you sense that stepping into this journey is the gateway to unlocking your true potential.

Meet Maya, a multitasking mother navigating the chaos of daily life. A whirlwind of energy juggling work, family, and her own aspirations. Amidst the hustle and bustle, she carved out moments of clarity like a seasoned sculptor, using simple yet effective methods to brave the storm.

Let's dive into Maya's world and unravel the methods and strategies she employed amidst life's chaos.

Maya knew that finding clarity wasn't just a luxury—it was a necessity amidst life's whirlwind. She craved those moments of peace and insight to guide her through the chaos.

First off, Maya embraced the power of journaling. Each morning, before the world woke up, she'd pour her thoughts onto paper, untangling the mess of her mind and setting intentions for the day ahead. It was her anchor in the storm, grounding her amidst the chaos.

But Maya didn't stop there. She also dabbled in mindfulness, stealing moments throughout the day to pause, breathe, and center herself amidst the chaos. Whether it was a quick meditation during her lunch break or a mindful walk in the evening, these small moments of stillness were her lifeline in the storm.

And let's not forget Maya's secret weapon: deep conversations. She made it a point to connect with trusted allies, diving into soul-searching discussions that sparked new insights and perspectives. It was in these moments of shared vulnerability that clarity often revealed itself, like a beacon in the fog.

So, there you have it—Maya's story of clarity strategies. Simple yet powerful, these techniques helped her navigate the storm of life with grace and intention, proving that amidst the chaos, clarity is always within reach.

Now, let's dive into the practical side of initiating your clarity quest. The key is finding methods that align with your personality and preferences. Whether it's journaling thoughts, diving into mindfulness, or deep conversations with trusted allies, there's no one-size-fits-all approach.

Remember, clarity isn't a quick fix; it's more like building Rome—one brick at a time. It's a journey of self-discovery, unfolding gradually. Give yourself permission to grow, trusting in the process.

As you navigate this journey, keep an open mind and a curious heart. Embrace challenges as opportunities, celebrating every small victory. And above all, keep your eye on the prize: uncovering the truth that sets your soul ablaze, leading to a life of purpose and fulfillment.

Reflective Question: Which approach strikes a chord with you for initiating your clarity journey, and how do you plan to weave it seamlessly into your daily routine?

Action Steps:

Step 1: Choose Your Path

Identify a method that speaks to your soul—whether it's journaling, mindfulness, or deep conversations.

Step 2: Dive In

Commit to incorporating this practice into your daily routine. Set aside dedicated time each day to engage with it, embracing it as a vital part of your growth journey.

Step 3: Stay Open

Remain flexible and open-minded as you explore. Be ready to adapt and adjust your approach as needed, trusting that clarity will reveal itself in unexpected ways.

1.6. Conquering Common Roadblocks on the Quest for Clarity

Alright, it's time to roll up our sleeves and tackle the hurdles that stand between us and clarity. Picture this: You're navigating through a dense fog of uncertainty, with obstacles lurking around every corner. But fear not—we've got the grit and determination to navigate these choppy waters and emerge victorious on the shores of clarity.

First, let's address the emotional rollercoaster of seeking clarity. It's like riding a wild bull—one moment, you're on top of the world, and the next, you're clinging on for dear life. But hey, that's all part of the adventure, right? Embrace the ups and downs, channel that energy into your quest, and watch as clarity starts to peek through the fog.

Meet David, a young professional who found himself at a crossroads in his career. Despite his passion for work, he constantly battled self-doubt and imposter syndrome, hindering his pursuit of clarity. It wasn't until he embraced vulnerability and sought support from mentors that he began to break through the obstacles blocking his path to clarity.

Alright, let's dive into David's journey and see how he kicked self-doubt to the curb with a dash of vulnerability and a sprinkle of resilience.

Now Picture this: David, a passionate professional, found himself at a career crossroads, wrestling with a gnarly beast called self-doubt. Instead of letting it steamroll him, he decided to face it head-on, armed with nothing but his courage and a hunger for clarity.

David knew deep down that he deserved more than sleepless nights filled with uncertainty. He craved a career that lit him up inside, one that aligned with his passions and values. And he well knew that letting self-doubt call the shots wasn't gonna get him there.

You ask now, what did David Do? Listen up Folks, First things first, David reached out for help. None of that lone wolf nonsense for him. He knew that vulnerability was his superpower, so he bared his soul to mentors and trusted friends, laying his struggles out on the table.

Then came the hard part: facing his demons. David stared self-doubt in the eye and said, "Not today, buddy." He dug deep, reflecting on his passions, strengths, and dreams until clarity started to poke its head out from behind the clouds.

Sure, it wasn't all rainbows and unicorns. There were plenty of moments when David wanted to throw in the towel and crawl back into his comfort zone. But he kept pushing forward, knowing that the discomfort of growth was a small price to pay for a life filled with purpose and meaning.

And you know what? It paid off. With each step forward, David gained clarity and confidence in his path. He embraced uncertainty as a natural part of the journey, trusting that the universe had his back every step of the way.

In the end, David emerged from the fog stronger and more grounded than ever before. He found a career that set his soul on fire and lit up the world around him, all because he had the courage to stare self-doubt in the face and say, "Not today, buddy. Not today."

Isn't it amusing how we often sabotage ourselves when seeking clarity? We build elaborate fortresses of procrastination and self-doubt, all in the name of avoiding the hard truths. But let's not take ourselves too seriously; sometimes, a good laugh at ourselves is just what we need to break down those walls and let the light in.

So, let's approach these obstacles with the resilience of a seasoned warrior. We'll face them head-on, armed with courage and humor; after all, the path to clarity isn't always smooth sailing, but we can navigate even the stormiest seas with the right mindset.

Reflective Question

Alright, let's journey back in time for a moment. Recall a time when self-doubt or uncertainty reared its ugly head in your pursuit of a goal or dream. How did you handle the situation?

Reflect on the role vulnerability played in seeking support and guidance from others. What lessons did you learn from navigating through those choppy waters?

Action Steps

Step 1: Embrace the Awkwardness

Alright, buckle up, 'cause we're diving headfirst into the discomfort zone. Identify an area in your life where self-doubt or uncertainty is calling the shots. Got it? Now, muster up the courage to share those feelings with someone you trust. Vulnerability isn't always easy, but it's the key to deeper connections and support.

Step 2: Seek Out the Wise Ones

Time to pick the brains of the wise sages in your life. Reach out to mentors, friends, or folks who've been down a similar road. Set up a coffee date or hop on a Zoom call to chat about your dreams and fears. Be open to soaking up their insights and wisdom like a sponge.

Step 3: Wrestle Those Demons

Alright, let's go toe-to-toe with those pesky thoughts that keep tripping you up. Challenge those negative beliefs with a hefty dose of positive affirmations and mindset shifts. Grab a journal, jot down your fears, and then flip 'em on their head with some empowering reframes.

Step 4: Get Your Butt in Gear

Enough talk, it's action time. Pick one tiny, itty-bitty step you can take today to move the needle on your goals. Whether it's sending that scary email or taking a leap into the unknown, just do it. Momentum builds with every baby step you take, my friend.

Step 5: Lean into the Discomfort

Newsflash: growth ain't always rainbows and butterflies. Embrace the discomfort and uncertainty as signs that you're leveling up. Lean into those moments with curiosity and courage, knowing that each hurdle you clear brings you one step closer to your dreams.

Step 6: Party Like It's 1999

Alright, it's time to break out the confetti and coffee. Celebrate every victory, no matter how small. Recognize the courage and resilience it took to face those inner demons head-on. You're a rockstar, and you deserve to pat yourself on the back for every milestone you crush.

1.7. Cultivating Self-Awareness to Unveil Life's Purpose

Join me on an inward journey where the landscape of the soul awaits exploration. Cultivating self-awareness is like embarking on an archaeological dig within ourselves, unearthing layers of experiences, beliefs, and emotions that shape our identity. It's a journey of introspection and self-reflection, guided by the light of curiosity and the desire to unearth the truth of our existence.

Imagine standing in the quiet sanctuary of your mind amidst the echoes of your thoughts and feelings. Here, in the depths of self-awareness, lies the key to unlocking the mysteries of our purpose. By peeling back the layers of conditioning and societal expectations, we reveal the raw, unfiltered essence of who we indeed are.

Meet Amy, a recent college graduate diving headfirst into a soul-searching expedition to uncover her life's purpose. Through mindful exploration and deep introspection, she unearthed dormant passions and values hidden by societal pressures. Her journey of self-discovery illuminated her path and empowered her to live authentically and intentionally.

Self-awareness invites us to embrace both the light and shadow aspects of ourselves, recognizing our strengths and weaknesses with humility and compassion. It's about acknowledging our deepest desires, fears, and aspirations and embracing them as integral parts of our being. In doing so, we gain clarity on what truly matters to us and how we can live a life aligned with our authentic selves.

Life has a way of injecting irony and absurdity into our moments of self-reflection. From the comical mishaps of our everyday lives to the unexpected revelations that catch us off guard, each experience adds a splash of color to the canvas of our self-awareness journey. In these moments of cheerfulness, we find solace and perspective, reminding us not to take ourselves too seriously as we navigate the complexities of existence.

As we traverse the landscape of self-awareness, we encounter both the light and shadow aspects of our being. We confront our fears, insecurities, and vulnerabilities with courage and compassion, knowing that actual growth arises from embracing our flaws and all. Through this process of self-discovery, we gain clarity on our values, passions, and purpose, paving the way for a life lived with authenticity and intention.

So, let us embrace the journey of self-awareness with open hearts and curious minds, knowing that each step brings us closer to unveiling the purpose that lies within. As we continue on this path of introspection and self-reflection, may we find joy in the exploration, wisdom in the revelations, and humor in the quirks of our humanity.

Reflective Question: Reflecting on your journey of self-awareness, what revelations have you unearthed about yourself, and how will you integrate this newfound understanding into your pursuit of life›s purpose?

Action Steps:

1. **Make Time for Reflection** – Take a moment each day to venture into your inner world. Whether it's a peaceful hike, writing in your journal, or practicing mindfulness, give yourself the space to explore your thoughts and emotions.
2. **Embrace Unvarnished Truth** – Confront the truths you've been avoiding—face them with honesty and vulnerability. Look at yourself in the mirror, metaphorically or literally, and discover what really drives you.
3. **Follow Your Passions**—Wholeheartedly Identify what truly sets your soul on fire and immerse yourself in those

activities. Whether it's dancing, painting, or hiking in nature, allocate time for what ignites your inner spark.
4. **Embrace Imperfections and Grow** – Acknowledge your flaws and mistakes with kindness. Instead of berating yourself, see them as lessons and stepping stones for your journey to becoming the best version of yourself.
5. **Foster Soulful Connections**—Surround yourself with people who uplift and inspire you on your path of self-exploration. Seek out mentors, friends, or online communities who share your passion for self-discovery and growth.
6. **Take bold action**—Use your newfound insights to propel you into action. Take bold risks, trust your instincts, and have faith that the universe will guide you as you embark on this exciting adventure called life.

1.8. Mindful Tech: Finding Balance in the Digital Jungle

1.8. 1. How to Stay Sane in a World of Screens and Notifications

Hey you, yeah, you with your eyes glued to the screen. It's time we had a little chat about this whole tech thing. Look, I get it. We live in a world where our phones are practically an extension of our bodies, where every beep and buzz pulls us deeper into the digital abyss. But here's the thing: we don't have to be slaves to our screens. We can take back control and use technology in a way that actually adds value to our lives. So buckle up, folks, 'cause we're about to embark on a journey to find some intentional and purposeful balance in this digital jungle.

1.8.2. The Double-Edged Sword of Tech

Alright, let's start with the basics. Technology? It's a double-edged sword, my friend. On one hand, it's revolutionized the way we live, work, and connect with one another. On the other hand, it's also turned us into dopamine-addicted zombies, constantly craving our next digital fix. So how do we navigate this minefield without losing our minds?

1.8.3. The Art of Mindful Tech Use

Welcome to Mindful Tech 101, my friend. This ain't your grandma's guide to turning off your phone and living in a cave. No, this is about using technology with intention, purpose, and, dare I say it, a little bit of absolute mindfulness. It's about asking yourself: "Is this tech adding value to my life, or is it just sucking away my precious time and energy?"

1.8.4. Setting Boundaries in a Boundaryless World

Alright, time to lay down some ground rules. You wouldn't let a wild animal run loose in your house, would you? So why do we let technology run roughshod over our lives? It's time to set some intentional boundaries, my friend. Put your phone on silent during dinner. Turn off notifications after 9 p.m. Take back control of your digital domain and watch as your sanity levels skyrocket.

1.8.5. Cultivating Digital Minimalism

Less is more, my friend. It's time to declutter your digital life and embrace the beauty of simplicity. Delete those apps you never use. Unsubscribe from those email newsletters that clog up your inbox. Streamline your digital existence until all that's left is what truly matters. Trust me, you'll thank me later.

1.8.6. Finding Purpose in the Digital Noise

Alright, let's get real for a second. What's the point of all this tech stuff anyway? Are we just mindlessly scrolling through Instagram for the rest of eternity? Hey no. We're using technology to enhance our lives, to pursue our passions, to connect with others in meaningful ways. So, listen up and ask yourself: "How can I use technology to live a more purposeful life?"

Reflective Questions

1. How has technology been impacting my daily life, both positively and negatively?
2. What are the areas of my life where I could benefit from more mindful and intentional tech use?
3. What changes can I implement today to achieve a better balance between digital engagement and purposeful living?

Action Steps

1. Identify Your Digital Triggers

Alright, champ, it's time for some brutal honesty. Take a good, hard look at your daily tech habits. What apps or notifications pull you into the digital vortex? Is it Instagram? Those incessant email pings? Identify your biggest digital distractions. Once you've got them in your sights, you can start to reclaim your time and sanity. Remember, awareness is the first step towards change.

2. Set Non-Negotiable Tech-Free Zones

Listen up, warrior. It's time to set some boundaries that even the nosiest of apps can't penetrate. Create sacred tech-free zones in your life. Start with something simple: no phones at the dinner table. Make your bedroom a sanctuary of rest, not a second screen. And for the love of all that's holy, turn off those notifications after 9 p.m. Trust me, the world will survive without you for a few hours.

3. Embrace Digital Minimalism

Alright, minimalist in training, here's your mission: declutter your digital life. Go on an app purge—if you haven't used it in the last month, it's toast. Unsubscribe from those spammy newsletters and streamline your social media to only follow what truly inspires you. This is your digital spring cleaning. Make it count. The goal here is to strip down your digital existence to the essentials, so every time you reach for your phone, it's intentional and valuable.

Reflect, simplify, and reclaim your digital domain. You've got this.

Conclusion: Alright, buddy, it's time to put your hands to work and start writing. Whether you choose the old-school method of pen to paper or the modern approach of typing on a keyboard, the important thing is to take action and begin expressing your thoughts and ideas. So, don't waste any more time contemplating, just dive in and start creating!

Choose one area of your life where you feel technology is having a negative impact and commit to implementing one mindful tech practice to address it. Remember, small steps lead to big changes. You got this.

1.9. Digital Detox: Finding Clarity and Purpose in an Age of Distraction

In a world that's constantly buzzing with notifications and updates, it's easy to get lost in the chaos. Yo, sometimes you gotta disconnect from all that tech stuff and take a step back to really find your purpose and get some clarity in life. It can be a total game-changer, you know what I'm saying.

Listen up, folks! This is your chance to shut off the constant buzz of the digital world and focus on what really matters: yourself and your values. And let me tell you, the research doesn't lie—taking a break from technology can drop your stress levels by a whopping 50% and give you a 30% boost in sleep quality. So what are you waiting for? It's time to unplug and recharge!

That's right, a digital detox, which is a period of time during which you refrain from using digital devices, can be just what you need to recharge and refocus. It's a chance to disconnect from the distractions of the digital world and reconnect with yourself and your values.

Hey there, I can totally understand what's going through your mind right now. "How can I possibly survive without my phone for a day?" But trust me, it's not as tough as it seems. You have the power to start small by turning off notifications or setting aside specific times to check your email and social media. It's about taking control of your digital life, not letting it control you. You'll be surprised at how liberating it can feel.

Taking a break from the digital world can be a refreshing and enlightening experience. Engaging in a digital detox can provide a unique chance to reflect on your life and contemplate your aspirations. It's crucial to ponder over questions like "What are your priorities?" and "How can you ensure that your actions are in line with your values?" during this time. This period can be utilized to build healthy habits and routines that will support your objectives and boost your overall well-being.

But don't just take my word for it. Give it a try for yourself and see how it feels. You may be surprised at how much you enjoy the peace and quiet. And who knows, you may even uncover a new passion or interest that you never had time for before. It's a journey of self-discovery and personal growth that awaits you.

Now that you've learned about the benefits of a digital detox, it's time to take action. Here are some reflective questions designed to help you think deeply about your digital habits, and here are actionable steps that you can implement to initiate your digital detox.

Reflective Questions: What are the biggest distractions in your life? How much time do you currently spend on digital devices each day? What activities or hobbies have you been wanting to try but haven't had time for?

Action Steps: Choose a day to disconnect from technology for a set amount of time (e.g., one hour, half a day, or a full day).

Set boundaries for technology use during mealtimes, before bed, or other times of the day when you want to disconnect. For instance, you can designate your bedroom as a technology-free zone, or commit to not checking your phone during meals.

Try a new hobby or activity that doesn't involve technology, such as reading a book, going for a walk, or practicing yoga. You could also try your hand at painting, gardening, or cooking a new recipe.

Remember, a digital detox doesn't have to be an all-or-nothing approach.

Start small and work your way up to longer periods of disconnection. Reflect on your journey and the benefits you've experienced along the way. By incorporating a digital detox into your routine, you can find clarity and purpose in an age of distraction.

In conclusion, by incorporating a digital detox into your routine, you can find the peace and clarity you need to live your best life. It's not just about disconnecting from technology, but also about reconnecting with yourself and your values.

Hey, why not take a shot at it? You might just be amazed at how it can shift your outlook and enhance your general state of mind.

1.10. Seeking Guidance from Mentors or Counselors

Now, let's explore the invaluable role of mentors and counselors in our journey to clarity and purpose. Imagine this: Jake, a young professional, was at a crossroads in his career. Despite his best efforts, he felt stuck and needed help deciding which path to take next. That's when he decided to seek guidance from a mentor.

Jake's mentor, Liz, had years of experience in the industry and a wealth of wisdom to share. Liz listened attentively to Jake's concerns in their conversations, offering empathetic support and practical advice. She helped Jake better understand his strengths, passions, and values, guiding him onto a career path aligned with his true purpose.

Similarly, consider Myra, who was navigating a challenging period in her personal life. Feeling overwhelmed by her emotions, Myra sought counseling to gain clarity and perspective. Myra found a safe space in her sessions to explore her thoughts and feelings, free from judgment. With the support of her counselor, Myra developed coping strategies. She gained valuable insights that helped her move forward with confidence and resilience.

These stories highlight the importance of seeking guidance from mentors and counselors when faced with uncertainty or confusion. Whether in our professional or personal lives, having someone to offer perspective, wisdom, and support can make all the difference in our journey towards clarity and fulfillment.

By tapping into their wisdom and experience, we can uncover blind spots and identify growth opportunities. Seeking guidance from mentors or counselors provides a fresh perspective on our challenges and helps us gain clarity on our goals and aspirations.

So, if you ever feel lost or need clarification, contact a trusted mentor or counselor. Their guidance and expertise can help illuminate your path and empower you to navigate life's trials confidently and clearly.

In today's fast-paced world, it's easy to feel overwhelmed and directionless. Seeking guidance from mentors or counselors is taking a proactive step towards personal and professional development. It is not a sign of weakness. It empowers us to make informed decisions and chart a course towards fulfillment and success.

Unexpected twists and turns abound in life's journey, yet it also offers moments of levity and humor. Seeking guidance may appear daunting, but it's also a chance to infuse humor into our path and refrain from taking ourselves too seriously.

Seeking guidance from mentors or counselors often arises from a mix of emotions—curiosity, fear, hope, and vulnerability. It's okay to feel uncertain or apprehensive. Still, it's also important to acknowledge the courage to reach out for support.

Challenging conventional wisdom and seeking guidance from mentors or counselors prompts us to question our assumptions and beliefs about success and happiness. It encourages us to explore new possibilities and embrace alternative paths to fulfillment.

Approach relationships with an open mind and ask for guidance when needed. Seek feedback and apply suggestions.

Reflect on your own journey:– Have you ever sought guidance from a mentor or counselor? What insights did you gain, and how did it impact your personal or professional growth? Consider leveraging mentorship or counseling to overcome challenges and achieve your goals.

As we dive deeper into the transformative power of mentorship and counseling, let's uncover the hidden gems of wisdom and insight that await us on this journey.

Action Steps:

1. Find Your Yoda
   Alright, padawan, it's time to get yourself a Yoda. In this context, a 'Yoda' refers to a mentor or guide, someone who can provide you with wisdom and guidance. Look around your professional and personal circles—who's got the wisdom you crave? Reach out to someone whose career or life you admire and ask them to be your mentor. It might feel awkward initially, but remember, even the greatest Jedi needed a mentor to show them the way. So, muster up that courage and shoot them a message. You'll be surprised how many wise folks are willing to share their knowledge.

2. Embrace the Couch Therapy Sessions
   Feeling like life's got you in a chokehold? It's time to hit the couch—no, not for Netflix binging, but for some good ol' counseling. Look out for a professional counsellor who can hand hold you untangle that mess of thoughts in your head. Therapy isn't just for when things are falling apart; it's also for when you need a tune-up. Think of it as taking your mind in for a service. Lay it all out there, get some perspective, and walk out feeling lighter, clearer, and more at peace.

3. Laugh at Your Struggles
   Life's a comedy, not a tragedy. When you're seeking guidance, don't forget to bring along your sense of humor. Seriously, lighten up. Talk about your struggles with a bit of levity. For instance, you could share your ridiculous career

dilemmas like accidentally sending a personal email to your boss or personal crises like getting lost in your own neighborhood. Watch as they become less daunting. Your mentor or counselor has probably heard it all and then some. So, don't be afraid to laugh at your own expense. It's the best way to keep your sanity intact while you're figuring out this crazy journey called life.

Embracing the Continuous Nature of the Journey Towards Clarity

Ever feel like you're chasing an illusion in the desert of life, always seeking clarity but never quite reaching it? Picture this: Richa, amidst shifting sands and shimmering horizons, learns a profound truth—that the quest for clarity is not a sprint but a marathon, a continuous journey with no finish line in sight.

Richa's journey—the recent college graduate who thought she had it all figured out, only to realize that life had other plans. As she embarked on her quest for clarity, Richa learned that the journey isn't about reaching a final destination but embracing growth and self-discovery.

In our pursuit of clarity, it's crucial to understand that the journey is not a one-time endeavor but a continual process of growth and discovery. Imagine Richa's journey—a winding path marked by moments of revelation and introspection. Each step she takes unveils new insights, propelling her to understand her purpose in life.

Like Richa, who stumbled upon unexpected oases of insight amid the vast expanse of ambiguity, we too can find moments of clarity in the most unlikely places, for every twist and turn offers an opportunity for growth and revelation.

The journey may sometimes feel daunting, filled with moments of doubt and confusion. But in these moments of uncertainty, we discover our resilience and inner strength. By embracing the continuous nature of our quest, we cultivate the courage to face whatever challenges come our way.

Recognizing the perpetual nature of our journey reminds us that clarity is not a fixed destination but a lifelong pursuit. It encourages us to embrace change and uncertainty as opportunities for learning and self-discovery. By embracing the fluidity of our path, we cultivate resilience and adaptability, essential qualities for navigating life's challenges.

Embracing our journey's ever-evolving nature requires cultivating a mindset of curiosity and openness. It involves letting go of the need for certainty and embracing the unknown with courage and humility. By remaining receptive to new experiences and insights, we empower ourselves to navigate the twists and turns of life with grace and resilience.

So let us not be discouraged by life's ever-shifting sands but rather inspired by the infinite possibilities that lie ahead. For in embracing the journey, we discover not only clarity but also the richness and depth of our own existence.

Reflective Question: How can you embrace the continuous nature of your journey towards clarity, and what steps will you take to navigate the uncertainties along the way?

Now, for some **Action Steps:** Take a moment to reflect on your own journey towards clarity. What obstacles have you encountered along the way, and how have you overcome them? What insights have you gained, and how will you apply them moving forward?

As we conclude our exploration of Chapter 1, let us carry forward the understanding that clarity is not a destination but a journey. This journey unfolds with each moment we embrace. In the next chapter, we dive deeper into exploring identity, uncovering the layers of our authentic selves, and embracing the transformative power of self-awareness. So, let's embark on the following pages with curious minds, ready to embrace what awaits us.

CHAPTER 2

DISCOVERING IDENTITY: UNVEILING YOUR ROLE IN THE WORLD

*E*ver felt like you're trying to navigate through a foggy maze, searching for the elusive key to your identity? It's a journey we all embark on, filled with twists, turns, and unexpected discoveries. Welcome to Discovering Your Identity—a quest to unveil your role in the world and find your place amidst the chaos.

Picture this: You're standing at a crossroads, pondering the question of who I am, who you are, and what you are meant to do in this vast world. You are not alone. This question is daunting and exhilarating, sparking a fire within you to seek answers and forge your path.

Let me share a story with you. Meet Alex, a recent college graduate struggling with the pressure to conform to societal expectations while also yearning to carve out a unique identity. Through a series of unforeseen encounters and thoughtful moments, Alex begins peeling back the layers of conditioning and discovering the essence of who they are.

Amid life's complexities, it's essential to maintain clarity about our identity. By stripping away the noise and distractions, we can uncover the core values, beliefs, and passions that define us.

Why does this matter, you ask? Because understanding our identity is the cornerstone of personal growth and fulfillment. It shapes how we perceive ourselves and interact with the world, influencing every aspect of our lives.

Ever notice how we sometimes get so caught up in pursuing our identity that we forget to enjoy the journey? It's like trying to find your way through a funhouse maze—frustrating at times, but ultimately a source of laughter and amusement.

As we explore identity, it's important to acknowledge the rollercoaster of emotions that accompany the journey. From self-doubt to bursts of confidence, each emotion offers valuable insights into who we are and what truly matters to us.

Here's a radical idea: What if our identity isn't fixed but somewhat fluid, evolving with each new experience and revelation? This notion challenges traditional notions of identity and invites us to embrace change as an integral part of self-discovery.

Reflection: So, where do we begin? Start by taking a moment to reflect on your own journey of identity exploration. What values and beliefs resonate with you? What passions ignite your soul? By embracing these aspects of yourself, you'll be one step closer to uncovering your true identity.

As we explore identity, remember that this journey is just beginning. With each step forward, you're inching closer to unveiling your authentic essence and role in the world.

2.1. Defining the Concept of Identity

Have you ever paused to ponder what makes you, well, you? It's a question that seems simple on the surface but unravels into a web of complexities as we explore deeper.

Picture this: You're sitting in a bustling coffee shop, sipping your favorite brew, when suddenly, the question hits you like a bolt of lightning—"Who am I?" It's a question that reverberates in the depths of your soul, urging you to define the very essence of your being.

Now, let me amuse you with a tale that might tickle your funny bone. Meet Emily, a quirky artist with a fondness for painting abstract landscapes. As she grapples with the concept of identity, she finds herself doodling furiously on her sketchpad, trying to capture the elusive essence of who she truly is. Through her whimsical incidents and thoughtful considerations, Emily embarks on a journey of self-discovery unlike any other.

But I digress. Let's come back to the heart of the matter—defining identity. At its core, identity transcends mere labels or traits. It's like a colorful quilt made up of our experiences, beliefs, and values, stitching together who we are and how we see ourselves in the world.

Now, you might be wondering, why does defining identity even matters. Well, my friend, it matters because it lays the foundation for everything else in our lives. From the way we interact with others to the choices we make, our sense of identity influences every aspect of our existence.

But here's the kicker—identity isn't set in stone. It's like a river, constantly flowing and changing course as we journey through life. Shaped by the currents of our experiences and the rocks of our interactions, our sense of self is constantly in flux. So, while defining our identity is crucial, we must also be open to the twists and turns that come with growth and evolution.

Ever notice how humans can spend hours agonizing over their identity, only to realize that it's as elusive as a unicorn? It's like trying to catch a cloud with your bare hands—you might get close, but you'll never quite grasp it.

Identity isn't a fixed construct but rather a fluid, ever-evolving concept. Embracing this fluidity allows us to adapt and grow with each new experience rather than clinging to rigid definitions of who we are.

So, as we navigate through the murky waters of identity, let's keep our spirits light and our minds open. Remember, discovering who we are isn't about uncovering a fixed destination; it's about embracing the constantly shifting landscape of ourselves with curiosity, humor, and genuine authenticity.

Reflective Question: Consider this: What aspects of your identity have been shaped by your upbringing and experiences? (how your past and present circumstances have shaped your identity) and envision how it will evolve.

How do these factors influence your perception of yourself and your role in the world?

Take a moment to reflect on how your past and present circumstances have shaped your identity.

Action Steps:
1. Start a journal to explore your thoughts and feelings about your identity.
2. Engage in activities that challenge your perceptions and broaden your understanding of yourself.
3. Seek feedback from trusted friends or mentors to gain insights into how others perceive you and your identity.

2.2. Exploring the Interconnectedness Between Identity and Purpose

Have you ever wondered how your identity shapes your purpose in this world?

In life's grand journey, our identity and purpose are intertwined like threads in a vibrant fabric. Each of us brings a unique blend of experiences, passions, and quirks, shaping our understanding of who we are and what we're here to do.

In this exploration, we'll dig deep into the heart of what makes us—who we are and how that shapes the path we tread. It's a journey of self-awareness and intentionality, where every revelation brings us closer to understanding our unique role in the grand scheme.

Take Rhea, for example. Growing up, she always felt a pull towards the arts – painting, dancing, writing. But society told her she needed to pursue a "practical" career path. So, she buried her creative passions beneath a pile of spreadsheets and reports, feeling unfulfilled and disconnected from her true self.

Have you ever experienced the frustration of trying to fit a square peg into a round hole? It's like trying to force something to fit where it doesn't belong - talk about a recipe for disaster!

Rhea's journey reminds us of the emotional toll of living out of alignment with our true identity and purpose. It can leave us feeling adrift, like ships lost at sea, searching for that elusive sense of belonging and fulfillment.

But here's the kicker—our identity isn't set in stone. It's a dynamic, ever-evolving aspect of who we are, shaped by our experiences, relationships, and choices. And guess what? Our purpose evolves right alongside it, like two dancers moving in perfect harmony.

Reflective Question

So, take a moment to ponder: How does your identity influence your sense of purpose? Are there aspects of yourself that you've been neglecting or suppressing? And most importantly, how can you harness the power of your identity to uncover your true purpose in life?

Transitioning from this exploration of identity and purpose, let's gain deeper insights into the practical steps for uncovering our life's calling.

Action Steps:

Reflect on Your Passions: Take some time to identify activities or interests that ignite your passion and bring you joy. These could be hobbies, creative outlets, or causes that resonate with you deeply.

Reconnect with Your Authentic Self: Reflect on aspects of yourself that you may have neglected or suppressed due to societal expectations or external pressures. Embrace those parts of yourself and consider how you can integrate them into your daily life.

Set Intentions: Define your core values and intentions for a purposeful life. What do you want to contribute to the world? What legacy do you want to leave behind? Setting clear intentions can guide your actions and decisions towards saligning with your purpose.

2.3. Assessing the Influence of Environment on Identity Formation

Have you ever stopped to think about how the world around you shapes who you are? It's like being sculpted by invisible hands, molding us into the individuals we become. Our environment profoundly impacts our identity, influencing us as individuals and shaping our personalities. From the communities we belong to the beliefs we hold, every aspect of our surroundings leaves its imprint on our sense of self.

Take Tom's story, for instance. He was raised in a bustling city where success was measured by wealth and status. Tom felt the pressure to conform to the norms of his environment, but deep down, he longed for a simpler, more fulfilling life aligned with his values and beliefs. Despite the challenges, Tom eventually found a way to create a supportive environment that nurtured his authentic self and helped him achieve his goals.

Our environment can be both a source of empowerment and a hindrance to our growth. It's like the water in which a fish swims, shaping our perceptions and influencing our worldview. But here's the kicker—we have the power to shape our environment, too. By being mindful of the people and things we surround ourselves with, we can create a positive and empowering environment that supports us in achieving our goals.

So, take a moment to reflect on how your environment has influenced your sense of identity. Are there aspects of your surroundings that empower you to be your authentic self, or do they hold you back from expressing who you indeed are? And most importantly, what changes can you make to create a more supportive environment that aligns with your values and aspirations?

Reflective Questions

1. How has your environment influenced your sense of identity?
2. Do aspects of your surroundings empower you to be your authentic self, or do they hold you back from expressing who you indeed are?
3. What changes can you make to create a more supportive environment that aligns with your values and aspirations?

Action Steps:

1. Reflect on Influences: Set aside some time to ponder the people, places, and moments that have shaped who you are today. Write down their significance and how they've impacted your sense of self.
2. Align with Values: Pinpoint any aspects of your surroundings that don't align with your values or goals. Develop a plan to address these inconsistencies, whether it's changing your environment or adjusting your approach.
3. Surround Yourself with Upliftment: Surround yourself with people and experiences that uplift and motivate you. Seek out communities that resonate with your values and beliefs, fostering a supportive environment for growth.

Remember, it's crucial to stay aware of how your surroundings influence you. Stay mindful and attuned to your environment, making adjustments as needed to ensure it supports your journey towards becoming the best version of yourself.

2.4. Recognizing the Impact of Cultural and Societal Factors on Identity

Hey there, friend! Have you ever stopped to think about how the culture and society you're born into shape the person you become? It's a big question but an important one to ask. The norms and beliefs we're exposed to during our upbringing exert a significant impact on our identity, and it can be a daunting task to liberate ourselves from those limitations.

Take Vera's story, for example. She grew up in a community where tradition and conformity were everything, leaving her feeling trapped in a role she didn't choose for herself. From a young age, she is taught to adhere to strict gender roles and expectations, stifling her individuality and autonomy. Despite feeling a deep longing to break free from these constraints, Vera struggled to reconcile her desire for independence with the pressures of her cultural upbringing.

Here's the thing, folks, you don't have to get stuck in that same situation. Remember, cultural and societal norms don't have the final say in who you are. You have the power to challenge the status quo and shape your own identity. It's like being handed a script for a play—you can improvise and make the role your own. So, take some time to reflect on how your own cultural and societal upbringing has shaped your identity. Are there aspects of that upbringing you've accepted without question but now feel compelled to reevaluate? Once you've identified those areas, think about how you can balance honoring your heritage with forging your path in life.

Reflective Questions

1. How have cultural and societal factors shaped your identity?
2. Are there aspects of your upbringing or environment you've accepted without question but now feel compelled to reevaluate?
3. How can you navigate the delicate balance between honoring your cultural heritage and forging your own path in life?

Action Steps:

1. Reflect on Influences:
   - Take time to ponder your upbringing and the societal norms shaping your identity. Write down your reflections for clarity.

2. Reevaluate Your Environment:
   - Identify any unquestioned aspects of your upbringing or environment and consider why you feel compelled to reassess them. Determine changes you wish to make.

3. Seek New Perspectives:
   - Explore diverse experiences and viewpoints to challenge your beliefs. Engage in activities like

reading, watching documentaries, or conversing with individuals from different backgrounds.

2.5. Embracing Diversity and Individuality in Identity Exploration

Listen up, my friends! It's time to ditch the societal norms and celebrate what makes us unique. Who wants to be a boring old circle when you can be a funky square peg?

Have you ever wondered why we're so quick to conform to societal norms instead of celebrating our unique quirks and differences? Well, it's high time we flipped the script and embraced the beauty of diversity and individuality in our journey of self-discovery.

Let's take Rachael, for example. Growing up, she felt like a square peg in a world full of circles. She never quite fit in with the crowd and always marched to the beat of her own drum. But instead of hiding her quirks and trying to blend in, Rachael embraced her individuality, and it led to a wild ride of chaos, confusion, and good times. The result? It was like trying to herd cats in a room full of dogs—chaos, confusion, and a whole lot of fun! And let's face it, who doesn't want a little bit of that in their life? So, have you ever felt gnawing like you're trying to squeeze into a pair of shoes two sizes too small? It's high time you flaunt those funky socks and strut your stuff.

The kicker is here: Embracing diversity isn't just about singing "Kumbaya" and holding hands. It's a gritty, down-to-earth journey that requires some serious elbow grease.

It's not just about our external differences like skin color, religion, or background. It's about the whole entirety—our experiences, perspectives, and identities. And trust me, my people, there's beauty in our differences and strength in our individuality. So, if you're feeling like a fish out of water, it's time to flaunt those fins and embrace your uniqueness. And while you're at it, let's create an environment that values and uplifts diversity.

Alright, listen up, folks Rachael's story is a testament to the power of embracing our uniqueness in a world that often pressures us to conform. It's about finding the courage to be unapologetically ourselves, even when it means going against the tide.

So, what's the takeaway here? Celebrate your quirks and embrace diversity in all its forms. Let's make the world a little more colorful, a little more chaotic, and a whole lot more fun!

Reflective Question

Here's a little food for thought: How can you celebrate your uniqueness and embrace the diversity around you? Are there aspects of yourself that you've been hesitant to share with the world? And most importantly, how can you foster an environment that values and uplifts the diversity of voices and perspectives in your community?

Do you ever feel like you don't fit in with the crowd? If you're ready to celebrate your own uniqueness and embrace the diversity around you, here are a few action steps you can take:

Action steps:

1. Yo, listen up, people! It's time to stop trying to be like everyone else and start embracing what makes you one-of-a-kind. Don't worry about fitting into society's boring mold. Instead, celebrate your quirks and let your unique personality shine. Just like Rachael did, it might lead you down a path filled with wild adventures, crazy scenarios, and loads of fun!
2. Challenge your biases, learn from others, create space for all voices to be heard, and take action to create a more inclusive world.
3. Foster inclusivity: Create an environment that values and uplifts diversity. Encourage open dialogue and create space for all voices to be heard.

2.6. Uncovering Hidden Talents and Strengths That Shape Identity

Yo, have you ever felt like you're just going through the motions of life without really knowing your purpose? Do you ever wonder if there's something more out there for you, some hidden talent or passion that you've yet to discover? If so, you're not alone, my friend. Many people go through life feeling unfulfilled, simply going through the motions of their daily routines without ever genuinely tapping into their full potential.

But what if I told you that a world of hidden talents and strengths lies dormant within you? Ah, the joy of uncovering hidden talents and strengths that shape who we are, just waiting to be unleashed? By embarking on a journey of self-discovery, you could find the unique gifts that shape your identity and propel you towards the life of your dreams.

Let me introduce you to Alex, a self-proclaimed "jack of all trades" who never quite found his niche in life. But one day, while tinkering away in their garage, Alex stumbled upon a knack for woodworking. What started as a hobby soon blossomed into a passion, unveiling a hidden talent that had been lying dormant within him all along.

Alex's story reminds us that our true talents and strengths often reveal themselves when we least expect them. It's like playing a game of hide-and-seek with your own talents—except instead of seeking, you stumble upon them while rummaging through life's clutter!

The journey of self-discovery is a complex one. It's filled with twists and turns, moments of surprise, excitement, and maybe even a bit of disbelief. But the secret is—uncovering our hidden talents isn't just about discovering what we're good at; it's about tapping into our passions and finding fulfillment in the process.

So, how can you embark on your own journey of self-discovery? The first step is to cultivate a mindset of curiosity and exploration.

Reflective questions: Start by asking yourself, What hidden talents or strengths do I suspect within me, just waiting to be unearthed? Are there activities or pursuits that bring me joy and fulfillment, but I've never considered pursuing them seriously?

Then, grant yourself the liberty to explore new experiences and endeavors, unshackled by the fear of falling short. Whether it's dabbling in a fresh hobby or tackling a novel project at work, dare to venture beyond your comfort zone and test your limits.

Finally, be patient and kind to yourself. Uncovering your hidden talents and strengths takes time and effort. Don't get discouraged if you don't find your passion right away. Remember, the journey itself is just as important as the destination.

Action Steps:

1. Set aside dedicated time for self-reflection and exploration. Experiment with new hobbies, activities, or experiences that pique your interest.
2. Reach out to those you trust—friends or mentors who know you well—and seek their honest feedback to pinpoint your areas of strength.
3. Embrace failure as part of the learning process and use it as fuel for growth. Stay open-minded and adaptable, allowing yourself the freedom to evolve and explore new passions.

Remember, the best thing you can give yourself is to surround yourself with people who let you live the life of your dreams!

2.7. Evaluating Personal Values and Beliefs That Define Identity

Have you ever been stuck at a crossroads, feeling as lost as a cat in a maze of laser pointers? Do you need help with your life's purpose? Are you struggling to align your actions with your values and beliefs? Well, don't worry; you're not alone. It's like we're all stuck in a maze, trying to find our way out, but instead of walls, our minds are blocking us.

Alright, folks, let's talk about something serious—core values and beliefs—the kind of stuff that defines who you are as a person. It's like being at a restaurant with a million options and suddenly realizing that what you really crave isn't even on the menu. Talk about an existential food dilemma!

Ah, It's time to get back on track and start living life on our own terms. First, let's identify our non-negotiable values and beliefs. What makes us tick? What brings us joy? What do we stand for? Write them down, scream them from the rooftops, or scribble them on your notepad—do whatever you like.

Next, let's evaluate our current actions and choices. Are they in harmony with our values and beliefs, or are we just going through the motions? Are we living authentically, or are we putting on a facade to please others?

Now, let me tell you a story about Emily. She's just like you and me, trying to navigate the demands of society while staying true to herself. And no, I'm not talking about taking a bunch of selfies and posting them on Instagram with a #self love caption (although, no judgment if that's your thing).

It's a bumpy ride, filled with doubts and uncertainties, but eventually, she finds clarity and conviction.

Emily's tale hits close to home for many of us, grappling with the tug-of-war between our inner truths and the outer noise of society. It's a wild ride, from questioning everything to finding solace in the eye of the storm.

But here's the key—it's not just about soul-searching. It's about taking ownership of your life and living authentically. It's about aligning your actions with your values, even if it means going against the norm. That's right—you gotta be a rebel, baby!

So, here's a riddle for you—let me ask you this—

Reflective Question: What are the non-negotiable values and beliefs that define who you are? Are you walking the walk, or are you just talking the talk? Are your actions and choices singing in harmony with these principles, or are they just off-key? And most importantly, how can you tune your life to hit all the right notes

Action Steps:

Carve out some quiet time to reflect on your core values and beliefs, jotting them down like a grocery list for the soul.

Take inventory of your daily decisions and behaviors, spotting any inconsistencies with your inner compass.

Channel your inner rebel and make bold moves to realign your life with your true self, whether it's saying "no" to that soul-sucking job or "yes" to that passion project you've been putting off.

Surround yourself with like-minded souls who get your vibe and support your journey towards authenticity.

Rinse and repeat because the journey of self-discovery is a never-ending road trip with plenty of pit stops for growth and exploration.

So my people, take some time to evaluate your core values and beliefs. And don't be afraid to make some changes if necessary. Remember, it's about living in harmony with your core principles, even if it means flipping society the bird.

So be true to yourself, and the rest will fall into place.

2.8. Overcoming Self-Doubt and Insecurities in Identity Discovery

Ever feel like you're tiptoeing through a minefield of self-doubt and insecurity, just waiting for one wrong step to blow up in your face? Let's throw some shade on those shadowy thoughts and learn how to kick those inner demons to the curb once and for all.

Let me introduce you to Rick, the master of all trades and the office king. His work ethic is so impressive, it makes the Energizer Bunny look ike a slacker. His sense of humor is so sharp it could cut through steel. Working with him is like being in the middle of a stand-up comedy show, except the jokes are funny. Trust me, you'll never have a dull moment with Rick around! But let me tell you this: Rick, also, like many of us, often grapples with feelings of inadequacy. Despite his impressive accomplishments, Rick frequently worries about his abilities and whether he measures up. It's like playing a never-ending game of "Guess Who?" with your own self-esteem, and it can be exhausting.

Rick's story resonates with many of us who face similar doubts and fears as we navigate life's challenges. It's a rollercoaster ride, with moments of confidence followed by periods of insecurity.

However, the good news is that overcoming self-doubt isn't about pretending those negative thoughts don't exist. Instead, it's about reframing our mindset and embracing our flaws and quirks. Vulnerability can be a strength in disguise, and by owning our imperfections, we can find a newfound sense of confidence and clarity.

So, get your thinking cap on, and let's get reflective. Here are three questions to ask yourself:

Reflective Questions:

What if our deepest insecurities were actually the keys to unlocking our hidden potential? How can we flip the script and turn self-doubt into a launching pad for growth and discovery?

How can we embrace our imperfections and vulnerabilities as badges of honor rather than sources of shame and embarrassment?

What practical steps can we take to cultivate a mindset of self-compassion and resilience, even when faced with the harshest critics—ourselves included?

Action Steps:

Keep a journal to track your thoughts and feelings when self-doubt comes knocking, shining a light on those dark corners of your mind.

Practice self-compassion like it's your full-time job, treating yourself with the same kindness and understanding you'd offer a needy friend.

Surround yourself with a squad of hype men and women who lift you and remind you of your worth, even on your darkest days.

Challenge your inner critic to a duel, armed with a self-affirmation sword and a resilience shield.

Remember, Rome wasn't built in a day, and neither is a fortress of self-confidence—it's a work in progress, so cut yourself some slack and enjoy the journey.

2.9. Seeking Feedback and Perspective from Trusted Individuals

In the grand adventure of life, seeking feedback and perspective from trusted individuals is like navigating with a compass in a dense forest—it helps us find our way when we're feeling lost.

Let me tell you a story about my friend Mark. He recently landed a job at his dream company, but he quickly realized that things were not what he expected. He was struggling to keep up with the culture and expectations, and he felt lost and hopeless. His work performance was also suffering, which made things even worse. Sounds similar, right?

One day, Mark's colleague Kim noticed that he was feeling down and asked him what was wrong. Mark hesitated at first, but eventually, he opened up to her about his struggles. Kim listened patiently and empathetically, and then she gave him some honest feedback about his work. She pointed out some areas where he could improve and some things he was doing well.

At first, Mark felt defensive and hurt, but as he thought more about Kim's feedback, he realized that she was right. He started implementing some of her suggestions, and he saw a significant improvement in his work and confidence.

From this experience, Mark learned the power of seeking feedback and perspective from trusted individuals.

Now, seeking feedback may feel like trying on a pair of jeans two sizes too small at first—uncomfortable and a bit awkward. But once you find the perfect fit, it's like discovering a treasure trove of insights you never knew existed. Mark's journey isn't just about improving his skills; it's about diving deep into the murky waters of self-awareness and emerging stronger and wiser on the other side. It's about recognizing that growth often requires stepping outside our comfort zones and embracing discomfort.

Reflective Questions: So, who are your trusted companions in this adventure we call life? Who are the ones you can count on to give you honest feedback, even when it stings a little? Cultivate those relationships and create a safe space for open and authentic communication. Remember, feedback isn't about criticism; it's about growth. So, embrace the discomfort, lean into the vulnerability, and watch yourself evolve into your best version.

Here are some **action steps** that you can take if you find yourself in a similar situation:

1. Identify the trusted individuals in your life whose feedback and perspective you value. These could be colleagues, mentors, friends, or family members.
2. Choose a trusted person and create a safe, non-judgmental environment when seeking honest feedback.
3. Be open to feedback, even if it's tough to hear. It's an opportunity for growth and self-discovery. Remember that feedback can provide valuable insights to help you grow and learn more about yourself.
4. Act on feedback by identifying areas for improvement and making changes in your behavior or actions. Reflect on your insights and use them to propel your self-discovery journey.

Seeking feedback is ongoing and requires vulnerability, but the rewards are worth it—self-awareness, improved performance, and deeper connections.

2.10. Celebrating the Journey of Self-Discovery and Identity Formation

Do you ever stand there, staring into the void, wondering what you are doing with your life? Well, let's raise a toast to the journey of self-discovery because it's time to celebrate your weird, messy, beautiful masterpiece.

Take Lily, for example. She's an excellent, innovative, talented, and unique artist who's been painting through life's ups and downs. Even though she's faced self-doubt and uncertainty, she's realized that her worth isn't tied to external achievements but to the authenticity of her creative expression.

Lily's story shows us that significance isn't about fitting into some predetermined box. It's about embracing the messy, imperfect journey of self-expression and finding joy in the process of becoming who you're meant to be.

Lily's journey of self-discovery has been nothing short of wild. Despite facing several setbacks and challenges, she has triumphed by realizing that her significance isn't linked to societal validation or external opinions. Instead, she has found it in the serene moments of self-reflection and self-acceptance. Furthermore, celebrating your own journey of self-discovery can be compared to throwing a surprise party for your soul. At the end of it, you are the special guest of honor.

All the stories we read remind us that significance isn't about flashy accomplishments or big gestures. It's about embracing the messy, imperfect journey of becoming who you're meant to be and finding joy in the small victories along the way.

But here's the thing: defining your significance in the world isn't a one-size-fits-all deal. It's about embracing your quirks, passions, and vulnerabilities and using them as fuel to light your path forward.

"Hey, people, it's essential to realize that your worth isn't determined by what others think of you. Instead, it's about being true to yourself and making a positive impact on those around you. The more authentic you are and the more you help others, the more valuable you become."

So, how do you define your significance in this ever-changing universe? Is it through your achievements, your relationships, or something else entirely?

As you reflect on your journey of self-discovery, how can you celebrate the weird, messy, beautiful masterpiece that is uniquely you? Because every moment, every experience, contributes to the bigger picture.

CHAPTER 3

TAKING CHARGE: DIRECTING YOUR LIFE'S COURSE

Oh, hello there, my friend! Are you feeling adventurous and excited to start an exciting self-empowerment expedition? Before we begin, let's take a moment to ponder: What does it mean to take charge in life? Imagine yourself at the helm of a ship, steering through the tumultuous seas of existence. It's not just about being in control; it's about embracing responsibility, making bold choices, and shaping your destiny.

Now, let me share a tale that might give you the inspiration you need. Meet Richa, a young professional who is feeling adrift in a sea of uncertainty. Despite her fears and doubts, she decides to take charge of her life by setting clear goals and taking decisive action. And boy, does she show us how perseverance and resilience can lead to discovering the power of self-direction and the freedom it brings.

But why does taking charge matter, you ask? It's simple, my dear: by embracing autonomy and ownership, we unlock our full potential and create the life we desire. No more aimless drifting, we become the captains of our fate, navigating towards our dreams with purpose and determination.

Now, here's the kicker: taking charge isn't just about seizing control; it's also about embracing the inevitable challenges and setbacks along the way. Life is full of unexpected twists and turns, but we can adapt, learn, and grow from every experience by taking charge.

"Friends, I am thrilled to share that these thought-provoking questions will act as our compass as we embark on this exciting journey. Let's dive deeper into this chapter and unlock the path towards a future filled with meaning and satisfaction."

Reflective Question: How do you envision taking charge of your life, and what steps can you take to start steering towards your desired destination? Oh, the possibilities!

3.1. Understanding the Concept of Taking Charge in Life

Have you ever felt like life is happening to you rather than you happening to life? It's a common sentiment, but what if I told you that you have the power to change that narrative? Welcome to the journey of taking charge in life—a path of empowerment and self-discovery.

Let's dive in with a relatable scenario: Meet Sarah, a young professional stuck in a job that doesn't fulfill her. Day after day, she finds herself going through the motions, wondering if this is all there is to life. Sound familiar? Many of us have been in Sarah's shoes, yearning for something more but unsure of how to break free from the status quo.

But here's the kicker: Taking charge in life isn't about making grand gestures or drastic changes overnight. It's about taking small, intentional steps towards creating the life you desire. It's about acknowledging that you have the power to shape your reality, no matter where you're starting from.

So why bother taking charge anyway? Well, for starters, it's about reclaiming your autonomy and agency. When you take charge of your life, you're no longer at the mercy of external circumstances or other peoples expectations. You become the captain of your own ship, steering towards the destinations that genuinely matter to you.

But here's the truth bomb: Taking charge also means taking responsibility. It means owning your choices, embracing the inevitable setbacks, and learning from every twist and turn along the way. It's not always easy, but it's undeniably worth it.

Now, let's get down to brass tacks. How do you start taking charge in life? It all begins with self-awareness and intentionality. Take a moment to reflect on what truly matters to you, what lights your soul on fire, and what you're willing to fight for. Then, muster up the courage to take that first step—no matter how small it may seem.

Reflective Question

As we explore taking charge in life, I invite you to ponder this: What areas of your life are calling out for your leadership? What steps can you take today to start steering towards a more fulfilling and purpose-driven existence? These questions will guide us on our journey of self-discovery and empowerment.

Action Steps:

1. Face the Brutal Truth

Alright, champ, time to confront reality. Take a good, hard look at your life. Which parts feel like they're stuck in a rut? Your job? Relationships? Personal goals? Identify the areas where you feel powerless. Acknowledge the dissatisfaction. Own it. This is the first step to taking charge—getting brutally honest with yourself about where you're at and why it sucks.

2. Embrace Micro-Movements

Forget about massive, life-altering changes for a second. Start with micro-movements. Want to switch careers? Begin by researching new fields or taking a relevant online course. Feeling unfulfilled in your personal life? Dedicate 15 minutes a day to a hobby you love. These tiny, intentional steps accumulate over time and create momentum. Remember, Rome wasn't built in a day, and neither is a kickass life.

3. **Commit to Radical Responsibility**

Here's the kicker: taking charge means taking full responsibility for your life. No more blaming your boss, your partner, or your circumstances. Everything that's happened up to now? Own it. This mindset shift is powerful. It puts you back in the driver's seat, giving you the control to steer your life in the direction you want. So, start making choices that align with your goals and values. Embrace the setbacks as lessons and keep pushing forward.

3.2. Assessing Personal Agency and Responsibility in Life Choices

Hey there, have you ever been at a crossroads in your life, feeling like the weight of your decisions could make or break your future? Yeah, me too. It's like being the captain of a ship, trying to navigate through stormy seas. You've got the power to steer your ship in any direction, but with that power comes a huge responsibility.

But let's be real: how often do we blame external factors for our problems instead of taking ownership of our own choices? It's easy to play the victim and blame fate for everything. But true empowerment comes from recognizing our agency and taking control of our decisions, no matter how scary they may seem.

For instance, my friend Stella had to choose between two job offers—one was safe and stable but offered limited growth opportunities, while the other was risky yet had more potential for growth. She struggled with the decision, but ultimately, she took ownership of her choices and decided to pursue the riskier option. And you know what? It paid off.

Our choices are like seeds that we plant in the soil of our lives. They have the potential to bear fruit and blossom into fantastic opportunities, or they can wither and die if we don't take responsibility for them. By embracing our agency and taking ownership of our decisions, we can navigate life's ups and downs with confidence and conviction.

So, how do we exercise our agency effectively? Well, start by being mindful and self-aware before making any decisions. Think about the potential consequences and take ownership of the outcomes, whether they're good or bad. Remember that proper growth and empowerment come from embracing your agency and taking responsibility for your life's direction.

Reflective Question: So, what about you? How do you define your action, and what steps can you take to exercise it more effectively in your life? Think back to your recent decision and consider how taking responsibility for the outcome influenced your growth and development.

Action Steps:

1. Take Full Ownership

Alright, it's time to stop pointing fingers and start owning your own life. Think back to a recent decision you made. Did it go south? Good. Instead of blaming your boss, your partner, or the universe, ask yourself: "What could I have done differently?" This isn't about beating yourself up—it's about learning and growing. Take ownership of your choices and their outcomes. It's the first step in realizing that you have the power to change your life.

2. Embrace Risk Like a Boss

Playing it safe might feel comfortable, but it's a surefire way to stagnate. Take a page out of Stella's book and start embracing calculated risks. Whether it's a career move, a personal project, or even a tough conversation you've been avoiding, lean into the uncertainty. Analyze the potential outcomes, make an informed decision, and then jump in with both feet. Remember, growth happens outside your comfort zone.

3. Cultivate Self-Awareness Daily

Self-awareness is your superpower, buddy. Start each day with a few minutes of reflection. Ask yourself: "What are my goals for today? How do my choices align with my long-term vision?" Journal your thoughts if you have to. This daily practice helps you stay connected to your true desires and ensures that your decisions are intentional. The more self-aware you become, the easier it is to exercise your agency effectively.

3.3. Cultivating a Growth Mindset to Embrace Change and Adaptation

Ever been caught in a whirlwind of unexpected changes, desperately clinging to the raft of routine, hoping it won't flip over? It's time to swap that leaky raft for a sturdy ship built on the foundation of a growth mindset—the ultimate tool for navigating life's choppy waters with finesse.

So, picture this: you're stuck in a downpour without so much as an umbrella to shield you. The rain is pouring down, and the wind is howling around you. You've got two options staring you in the face: cower under a tree like a soggy squirrel and pray for the skies to clear, or say forget it, kick off your shoes, and start grooving to the beat of the rain. Because let's face it, every droplet is a chance to soak up some fresh life lessons and grow from the experience. It's your call, buddy. How do you want to get drenched by life today?

Why does it matter, you ask? Well, let me tell you: a growth mindset is like the special ingredient that spices up both your personal and professional life.

Hey, friend! Life's a rollercoaster, isn't it? But here's the kicker: it's not about the highs, it's about how we tackle the lows that truly defines us. Instead of letting setbacks knock us down, we've got the power to see them as chances to level up, and obstacles as stepping stones to bigger and better things. It's all about flipping the script and turning adversity into opportunity. Cool, right?

This mindset? It's like having a superpower that turns every obstacle into a launchpad towards our dreams. When we keep our eyes on the prize and stay driven, even when the going gets tough, there's nothing we can't conquer. So, here's the deal: setbacks? They're just pit stops on the road to success, opportunities to level up and evolve. Let's tackle each challenge head-on, armed with optimism, and watch ourselves become the ultimate versions of who we can be!

Let me share a story with you. Meet Alisha, a young professional navigating the tumultuous waters of a rapidly changing industry. Alisha could have easily succumbed to fear and uncertainty when faced with unexpected challenges and setbacks. Instead, she chose to adopt a growth mindset, viewing each obstacle as an opportunity to learn and grow. Through resilience and perseverance, Alisha weathered the storm and emerged stronger and more resilient than ever before.

But how do we cultivate this mindset? It starts with shifting our perspective from "I can't" to "I can learn." It's about embracing the unknown with curiosity and resilience.

Here's the scoop: Life's a bit like a river, always on the move, constantly changing its course. So, instead of paddling upstream and exhausting ourselves, why not learn to surf those waves? Embracing change is all about riding the currents, going with the flow, and seeing where it takes us.

Reflective Question: Now, take a moment to mull over your own dance with change. When uncertainty comes knocking, do you tend to dig in your heels or go with the flow? Are there parts of your life where you could loosen up a bit, roll with the punches, and embrace the adventure with a more open mind?

Here's the deal: when we embrace change and nurture that growth mindset, we're unlocking a treasure trove of endless possibilities. So, why not dive headfirst into the unknown, knowing that every twist and turn in life's wild ride is a chance to level up? It's like embarking on an epic adventure with each curveball thrown our way—an opportunity to grow, evolve, and become the heroes of our own stories!

Action Steps:

1. Turn Failures into Lessons

Alright, let's be real. Life isn't all sunshine and rainbows. When you hit a bump in the road, don't see it as the end of the world. Instead, ask yourself: "What can I learn from this?" Each setback is a lesson in disguise. Missed a deadline at work? Great, now you know how to manage your time better next time. Start viewing these moments as stepping stones rather than stumbling blocks.

2. Embrace New Challenges

Curiosity didn't kill the cat; it made it smarter. When faced with something new and challenging, dive in headfirst with a curious mind. Don't shy away because it's unfamiliar. Ask questions, seek out new information, and embrace the discomfort. Got a new project that seems out of your league? Perfect. This is your chance to stretch your skills and grow. The more you tackle the unknown, the more confident and capable you'll become.

3. Be Patient with Yourself

Growth doesn't happen overnight, so cut yourself some slack. When things get tough, remember that patience and persistence are key. Celebrate small wins and remind yourself that progress is a journey, not a sprint. Reflect on how far you've come and use that to fuel your motivation. Facing a tough situation? Take a breath, remember your past successes, and keep pushing forward. You've got this.

By adopting these steps, you'll start to see challenges as opportunities, build resilience, and continuously improve in both your personal and professional life.

3.4. Setting Clear Goals and Intentions to Direct Life's Course

Yo, have you ever felt like you're just floating through life without a clue where you're headed? Like a lost sailor on a vast sea of uncertainty? I feel you, my friend. But fear not, for I've got some wisdom to drop on you that'll help you chart a course for your ship and steer it towards your desired destination with purpose and clarity.

Imagine you're standing at the helm of your ship, looking out at the horizon with determination in your eyes. Each goal you set is like a guiding star, illuminating the path ahead and steering you through the turbulent waters of life. Just like Jane, the young professional who got unstuck from her dead-end job by defining her goals and intentions and taking actionable steps towards them.

Now, let's get real. Setting goals isn't just about dreaming big; it's about breaking them down into smaller, achievable tasks and taking consistent action towards them. But life is unpredictable, and sometimes, we need to adapt and evolve our goals along the way. That's where flexibility comes in. We can stay agile and resilient in the face of adversity by staying open to change. So, how do we set clear goals and intentions?

It starts with looking inward and figuring out what we truly want out of life and what values and priorities matter most to us. Once we have that clarity, we can map out our goals and create a plan of action. And don't forget the power of accountability and celebrating our successes along the way.

Reflective Question: So, reflect on your own goals and intentions. What steps can you take today to move closer to achieving them? It could be making a to-do list, reaching out to a friend for support, or taking a small step towards that big dream. Whatever it is, take action, my friend. You got this!

Action Steps:
1. Look, if you want to achieve anything worthwhile in life, you gotta start by figuring out what you stand for.
2. What are your core values and priorities? Once you've got that down, then you can start setting goals that genuinely align with what matters to you.
3. But here's the thing: big goals can be overwhelming. That's why it's important to break them down into smaller, actionable tasks.
4. That way, you can make progress one step at a time and avoid getting bogged down.

And listen, life is unpredictable. You gotta stay flexible and be willing to adapt your goals as needed. Change is just part of the journey, my friend.

3.5. Understanding and Utilizing Your Strengths and Weaknesses in Directing Your Life

Ever feel like you're juggling more balls than a circus clown on caffeine? Yeah, me too. But what if I told you that the secret to mastering this chaotic circus act called life lies not in catching every ball perfectly but in knowing which ones to let drop and which ones to juggle with finesse? Intrigued? Let's dive in.

Picture this: You›re at a pivotal moment in your career, standing at the edge of uncertainty. The question looms: Which direction should you take? As you ponder, lets dive into the art of navigating life's twists and turns by harnessing the power of your strengths and acknowledging the quirks of your weaknesses.

Real-Life Story: Let's meet Kelly, a marketing whiz armed with creativity that could rival Da Vinci. She's a master at crafting compelling ad campaigns and has a knack for understanding consumer behavior. However, when it comes to public speaking, her knees turn to jelly, and her words stumble like those of a toddler learning to walk. Recently, Kelly found herself at a career crossroads. Should she pursue a role that emphasizes her strengths in marketing or challenge herself to overcome her fear of public speaking and explore new horizons? Let's see how she navigates this dilemma.

Kelly dive into understanding her strengths and weaknesses through introspection and feedback from colleagues and mentors. For instance, she reflects on her ability to devise innovative marketing strategies as a strength, while she acknowledges her fear of public speaking as a weakness.

She evaluates the opportunities before her, considering how her strengths can propel her forward while acknowledging areas for growth.

Kelly, like you, understands that embracing her strengths and addressing her weaknesses is not a sign of weakness, but a path to empowerment. By acknowledging her strengths, she can confidently take on tasks that align with her skills, leading to increased job satisfaction and career success. Similarly, by addressing her weaknesses, she can improve her overall performance and open up new opportunities for growth. It's about finding the right balance to steer her career towards fulfillment and success.

Reflective Questions:

- What are the unique strengths and weaknesses that shape your journey?
- How do they influence the choices you make in directing your life's course?
- Are you embracing your strengths fully or shying away from challenges due to your weaknesses?

Action Steps:

1. **Embrace the Journey of Self-Discovery:** Take a courageous step inward to uncover your unique strengths and weaknesses. Reflect on past experiences and the valuable feedback from others. This is where your growth begins, and your role in this process is invaluable.

2. **Evaluate Opportunities:** Consider how your strengths can propel you forward in your chosen path while also acknowledging areas where growth is needed. For example, if you're a great communicator, you could consider roles that require strong interpersonal skills. On the other hand, if you struggle with time management, you could look for opportunities to improve this skill.

3. **Find Balance:** Seek opportunities that allow you to leverage your strengths while addressing your weaknesses in a supportive environment. This balance is key as it will enable you to excel in areas you›re already strong in while also working on areas that need improvement.

4. **Invest in Growth:** Take deliberate steps to improve upon your weaknesses, whether it›s through training, mentorship, or personal development.

5. **Stay Agile:** Be open to feedback and adaptable to change. Remember, growth often requires stepping outside your comfort zone. This is where your true potential can shine. In the intricate weave of life, it's not about striving for flawlessness but about embracing the beautiful mess of who you are. Take Kelly, for instance. Armed with her

unique blend of strengths and weaknesses, she fearlessly ventures into the maze of life's possibilities, demonstrating her adaptability and open-mindedness.

So, my friend, regardless of where you are in your journey, grab hold of your compass, steel your resolve, and embark on the exhilarating journey of self-discovery. Your path is waiting, woven with threads of authenticity and resilience. It's time to unveil it and navigate with confidence.

3.6. Building Resilience to Navigate Through Life's Challenges

Ever felt like life was throwing curveballs at you left and right, leaving you wondering how to stay afloat amidst the chaos? Well, you're not alone.

Life has a knack for testing our resilience, presenting us with unexpected challenges that push us to our limits. But hold on because resilience is not just about weathering the storm—it's about harnessing your inner strength to navigate through life's toughest moments with grace and determination.

Picture Myra's tale: a single mom juggling multiple jobs to keep her family afloat. When one job vanished, she faced sudden financial setbacks, Myra could've drowned in despair. But fueled by her fierce love for her kids, she tackled setbacks head-on with grit and grace. Despite the punches, Myra pushed through, securing a new job that not only brought stability but also chances to thrive.

Now, think about Myra's journey. How does her resilience mirror your own battles? What nuggets of wisdom can you snatch from her playbook for your own life's hurdles?

Resilience isn't just about bouncing back; it's about rolling with the punches, staying true to yourself, and being focused on what truly matters. Myra's saga? A punchy reminder of resilience's mighty force in facing life's curveballs.

Growing resilience? It's a muscle you flex over time. Embrace change, stay nimble, and see setbacks as springboards for growth. That's how you strut through life's storms with swagger.

Myra's ride emphasizes the need for a support squad—friends, family, mentors—who have your back when the going gets tough. And remember perseverance? It's your secret weapon against life's sucker punches.

Resilience ain't some exclusive club—it's a muscle you can beef up with each hurdle you tackle. So, as you navigate the wild ride of self-discovery and growth, keep this in mind: your resilience? "It's your hidden strength," primed to knock out any curveball life lobs your way. Embrace it, feed it, and let it guide you through the choppy waters of uncertainty with fierce grit and courage. You're unstoppable!

Reflective Question: Have you ever wondered how you beef up your resilience? Take a cool stroll down memory lane to those tough times and mull over the tricks you used to conquer them.

Action Step: Take a peek at your support squad—your pals, fam, and mentors—and see how they've boosted your bounce-back power. How can you strengthen these bonds to up your resilience game when the going gets tough?

Remember, you're tougher than you think. With the right mindset and support crew, there's no storm you can't weather. Keep on shining!

3.7. Honoring Personal Boundaries and Asserting Control Over Life's Direction

Have you ever felt like life was pushing you in a direction you didn't want to go, leaving you feeling overwhelmed and out of control? It's time to take a stand and set your boundaries, steering your life with confidence and clarity.

Meet John, a young professional juggling work and personal life. Despite his best efforts, he ends up saying "yes" to everything, to additional projects and commitments, leaving him feeling exhausted and drained. It's not until he reaches a breaking point, experiencing burnout and resentment, that John realizes the importance of setting clear boundaries. But when he hits rock bottom, Ah! John realizes the power of boundaries. With newfound courage, he starts saying "no" to things that drain him. And guess what? He feels freer and stronger than ever before, experiencing a sense of freedom and empowerment, reclaiming control over his life's direction.

Boundaries aren't about being selfish; they're about taking charge of your life. John's tale shows how they transform your life for the better, aligning it with what truly matters.

So, let's talk about boundaries. They're the rules we set for ourselves, guiding how we interact with others and navigate the world. By establishing and enforcing healthy boundaries, we protect our emotional and physical well-being and deepen our connections with ourselves and others.

While setting boundaries may seem daunting at first. John's journey teaches us to know ourselves and speak up. It highlights the importance of self-awareness and assertiveness in setting and maintaining boundaries. By clearly communicating his needs and priorities, John effectively establishes boundaries that support his overall well-being and happiness. Even in tough times, a good laugh can break the ice and help us assert our boundaries with style.

Remember, setting boundaries isn't about shutting people out—it's about creating healthy relationships and fostering mutual respect. When we honor our boundaries, we communicate our standards for treatment to others, fostering an atmosphere conducive to authentic connections and personal development. Boundaries serve as bridges, not barriers. They're the secret to healthier relationships and a more authentic life. So, take the reins and steer your life with courage. You've got this!

Reflective Question: Consider a recent situation where somebody challenged your boundaries. How did you handle it, and what did you learn from that experience?

Quiz: Do you constantly say «yes» to additional commitments, even when stretched thin?

Action Step: Take a cue from John›s story and start asserting your boundaries. Politely decline requests that encroach on your personal time and well-being to reclaim control over your life›s direction.

3.8. Fostering Accountability in Decision-Making and Action-Taking

Imagine, you're faced with a critical decision that could alter your entire life. In that moment, what guides your choices and actions? It's the power of accountability—the driving force behind responsible decision-making and intentional action.

Meet Michele, a young entrepreneur embarking on a new business venture. As she navigates the challenges of entrepreneurship, Michele encounters numerous obstacles and setbacks along the way. However, instead of succumbing to self-doubt and indecision, Michele embraces accountability as her guiding principle. With each decision she makes, Michele takes ownership of the outcomes, whether successes or failures. By holding herself accountable, Michele cultivates a sense of empowerment and resilience, propelling her to her goals with unwavering determination.

Accountability is more than taking responsibility for our actions—it's about aligning our decisions and behaviors with our values and intentions. Michele's narrative demonstrates the transformative power of accountability in navigating life's challenges and pursuing ambitious goals.

In a world filled with distractions and external influences, accountability serves as a compass guiding us towards our desired destination. By fostering accountability in decision-making and action-taking, we empower ourselves to create the lives we envision and achieve our goals with purpose and integrity.

By embracing accountability, individuals like Michele can overcome obstacles with resilience and determination, ultimately realizing their full potential with the clarity and authenticity that come from owning our choices and remaining true to ourselves.

While the journey towards accountability may have its ups and downs, it's often through moments of levity and humor that we find the resilience to persevere. Laughter has a remarkable ability to alleviate the weight of responsibility and remind us not to take ourselves too seriously.

Taking accountability means being willing to face discomfort and uncertainty head-on and fully embracing the challenge while taking ownership of our triumphs and setbacks. By holding ourselves accountable, we enable growth and learning from every experience, ultimately becoming architects of our destinies.

Reflective Question: Think about a recent decision you made that had significant consequences. How did you approach the decision-making process, and what role did accountability play in your actions? Consider how to foster greater responsibility in your decision-making and action-taking moving forward.

Action Steps:

1. Set Clear Intentions: Define your values and intentions to align your decisions with your goals. Please write down your priorities and revisit them regularly to stay focused.
2. Own Your Choices: Take responsibility for your actions, whether they bring success or failure. Reflect on your decisions' results and learn from the triumphs and setbacks.
3. Find your support system: Seek Support. Surround yourself with individuals who encourage accountability and provide constructive feedback. Share your goals and progress with them to stay motivated and accountable.

Accountability isn›t just about admitting mistakes; it›s about steering your life with purpose and integrity. By embracing accountability, you empower yourself to navigate challenges and achieve your aspirations with resilience and determination.

3.9. Seeking Support Networks and Resources for Empowerment

In the grand adventure of life, we often find ourselves walking a tightrope, balancing dreams, responsibilities, and challenges with a delicate touch. But fear not, for in the midst of this swirling storm of uncertainty, there exists a lifeline that can bolster our spirits and fortify our resolve: support networks and resources.

Let's meet Karen, a single mother bravely juggling the demands of a bustling career and the joys of parenthood. Feeling the weight of her responsibilities pressing down, Karen reached out to a local community center that offered support groups for working parents. In these gatherings, Karen discovered a sanctuary where shared experiences brought solace, practical tips abounded, and emotional support flowed freely, helping her navigate life's complexities with newfound courage.

Look, we all need a little help sometimes. In today's interconnected world, support networks come in all shapes and sizes—from lively online forums and buzzing social media groups to cozy local community organizations and bustling professional associations. These networks aren't just safety nets; they're lifelines; they're the difference between feeling lost and alone and like we belong somewhere. They offer a sense of belonging and understanding and get us through the ups and downs of life's rollercoaster ride.

Individuals can tap into a treasure trove of knowledge, guidance, and empathy by actively seeking out and engaging with support networks and resources. These networks aren't just about surviving; they're about thriving. They empower us to face life's challenges head-on, armed with confidence and resilience.

In a society that often celebrates independence and self-sufficiency, it's crucial to understand the importance of seeking out support networks. It's about acknowledging that we're not navigating this journey alone—together, we're more resilient. By embracing these networks, we foster a feeling of empowerment and belonging that drives us towards achievement and contentment.

Reflective Questions:
1. Reflect on your own journey: What support networks or resources have been your saving grace in times of need?
2. How can you actively seek out and engage with support networks to enhance your sense of empowerment and resilience?
3. Looking back on your experiences, what pearls of wisdom or life lessons have you gained from your interactions within support groups or networks?

Action Steps:
1. Dive into Discovery: Take a plunge into exploring various support networks and resources that cater to your unique needs and aspirations.
2. Extend a Hand: Don't wait for support to come to you—reach out and actively participate in relevant support groups and communities, both online and offline.

3. Nurture Connections: Foster meaningful connections within your chosen networks by sharing your stories, seeking advice, and offering support to fellow travelers on this journey called life.

In the grand scheme of life, seeking support networks and resources isn't just about finding a shoulder to lean on; it's about finding a tribe that cheers you on, lifts you up, and walks alongside you every step. So, let's embark on this adventure together, armed with the power of community, resilience, and unwavering support. We've got this!

3.10. Embracing Flexibility and Openness to Opportunities Along the Journey

Life's journey resembles a turbulent sea, with change as its only constant. Amidst the unpredictable waves, it's not just about forging ahead with unwavering determination; it's about embracing the unexpected deviations and unexpected opportunities that come our way.

Consider the story of Kevin, a budding entrepreneur with a crystal-clear vision of his future. Along his path, Kevin encountered unforeseen challenges and surprising opportunities, demanding a shift in perspective and strategy. Rather than resisting change, Kevin embraced flexibility and openness, seizing new possibilities and adapting his approach to align with emerging opportunities.

Flexibility and openness aren't just admirable traits; they're essential survival skills in our fast-paced world. Those rigidly clinging to plans often find themselves blindsided by change, while the adaptable navigate challenges with grace and resilience.

By embracing flexibility and openness, individuals cultivate a mindset responsive to change and receptive to new opportunities. This mindset empowers them to pivot when necessary, seize unexpected possibilities, and chart a course aligned with evolving aspirations and values.

In a world where uncertainty reigns supreme, flexibility and openness are invaluable assets. Cultivating these qualities not only eases navigation through life's uncertainties but also unveils unforeseen paths to fulfillment and success.

Reflective Questions:

How will you realign your life with your purpose amidst life's unpredictable changes?

Reflect on your comfort level with uncertainty and change. Identify areas where flexibility and openness could enhance personal growth and success.

Recall a time when embracing flexibility led to unexpected positive outcomes. How can you apply those lessons to cultivate adaptability and resilience?

Action Steps:

1. Dedicate regular time for self-reflection to ensure actions remain aligned with purpose, adapting to changing circumstances.

2. Embrace uncertainty by seeking new experiences outside your comfort zone, fostering continuous growth.
3. Develop resilience by viewing obstacles as opportunities for personal development and learning.

As we journey through life's unpredictable waters, embracing flexibility and openness isn't merely about survival; it's about thriving amidst change and uncertainty. By fostering these qualities, we empower ourselves to seize unexpected opportunities and confidently navigate towards fulfillment and success.

CHAPTER 4

NAVIGATING CHALLENGES: OVERCOMING OBSTACLES ON YOUR PATH

*H*ave you ever felt like life's challenges were crashing your party, throwing off your plans, and leaving you feeling stranded? Yes, challenges and obstacles are inevitable in life. They often appear unexpectedly, like unwelcome guests disrupting our plans and testing our resolve. Well, fear not; you're not alone. "Hey there! Just a heads up, every challenge brings with it a chance to grow, become more resilient, and learn about yourself. So, get pumped for an exciting journey of overcoming life's obstacles with flair!"

Imagine yourself as a fearless explorer, boldly charting through the maze of challenges that life throws your way. From dodging the pitfalls of self-doubt to navigating unexpected twists and turns, this chapter is your trusty map to overcoming adversity like a pro.

But hey, it's not all serious business—buckle up to tackle obstacles like a boss. With a combination of humor, unwavering determination, and the insights gained from facing every difficulty, you will emerge as a more resilient, knowledgeable, and self-assured individual, equipped to handle any curveball that life may throw your way.

Let's Go!

4.1. Understanding the Nature of Life's Challenges and Obstacles

Have you ever felt like life was tossing one impossible hurdle after another, faster than you could keep up? You're not alone. Life's challenges come in many forms and sizes, each presenting its unique hurdles to navigate., from minor inconveniences to significant setbacks that shake us to our core. But what if I told you that these challenges hold the key to unlocking your full potential?

Imagine this: You're trekking up a steep mountain trail, each step a test of your strength and endurance. Along the way, you encounter obstacles—loose rocks, fallen branches, and sudden downpours—that threaten to derail your progress. Yet, with each obstacle overcome, you grow stronger, more resilient, and more determined to reach the summit.

Now, let's dive deeper into the nature of life's challenges. They often arise when we least expect them, catching us off guard and forcing us to adapt on the fly. But herein lies the beauty of adversity: it reveals our true character and pushes us to become the best versions of ourselves.

Consider the story of Debbie, a young professional navigating the competitive world of corporate finance. Just when she thought she had it all figured out, a global economic downturn sent shockwaves through her industry, leaving her jobless and uncertain about the future. Instead of succumbing to despair, Debbie embraced the challenge as an opportunity to reinvent herself and pursue her passion for entrepreneurship.

But why do challenges matter, you ask? Because they serve as catalysts for personal growth and transformation. By facing adversity head-on, we develop resilience, perseverance, and a newfound appreciation for life's journey.

So, how do we navigate life's challenges with grace and resilience? To tackle life's challenges with grace and resilience, we need to change our perception of obstacles. Instead of seeing them as roadblocks, we should view them as stepping stones that help us reach our goals and succeed.

Adopting this change in perspective enables us to tackle challenges with optimism and a relentless drive to prevail. We empower ourselves to overcome any obstacle that stands in our way.

Reflective Question: What lessons have you learned from past challenges, and how have they shaped your resilience and determination moving forward?

Action Steps:

1. Welcome the challenge: Rather than viewing obstacles as hurdles, perceive them as chances for personal development and exploration. Keep an open mind and be willing to learn from each experience.
2. Develop Resilience: Foster resilience by adopting a positive outlook and focusing on finding solutions rather than dwelling on problems. Draw inspiration from past triumphs and remind yourself of your capacity to overcome adversity.
3. Seek Assistance: Never shy away from relying on friends, family, or mentors for guidance and motivation during difficult periods. Surround yourself with a supportive community that inspires and motivates you to persevere.

Remember, challenges are not roadblocks but stepping stones on the path to success. Embrace them with courage and determination, Understanding that every obstacle conquered contributes to your strength and resilience.

4.2. Recognizing the Difference Between Internal and External Challenges

Ever wondered why some challenges leave us feeling defeated while others propel us to new heights of achievement?

Life tosses us with various challenges, but not all hurdles are alike. Some arise from forces beyond our grasp, while others originate from within, lurking like hidden traps in the corridors of our minds. Understanding the contrast between internal and external challenges is critical to navigating life's twists and turns with resilience and clarity.

Let's embark on a voyage to unravel the intricacies of internal and external challenges through real-life tales. Picture yourself training for a marathon, a daunting journey demanding physical stamina, mental grit, and unyielding resolve. As you pound the pavement day after day, you confront both internal and external obstacles that test your mettle.

External challenges manifest as physical barriers—think unpredictable weather, rugged terrain, and congested running paths. These factors lie beyond your sphere of influence, yet they wield significant sway over your training routine and overall performance.

On the flip side, internal challenges spring from within, born of your thoughts, beliefs, and emotions. Self-doubt, fear of failure, and waning motivation are common internal hurdles capable of sabotaging your training endeavors and impeding progress. While these challenges may not be as tangible as external ones, their effects can be equally profound, if not more so.

Enter Naomi, a devoted marathoner gearing up for her inaugural ultramarathon. Despite her meticulous preparation and rigorous training regimen, Naomi finds herself grappling with internal demons that threaten to derail her quest. As the race looms closer, she wrestles with self-doubt and impostor syndrome, questioning her ability to conquer the daunting distance ahead.

Yet Naomi refuses to let her internal struggles dictate her destiny. Through introspection, resilience, and the unwavering support of her community, she learns to acknowledge her fears and insecurities while fostering a mindset of self-compassion and resolve. With each stride towards race day, Naomi confronts her inner adversaries head-on, emerging stronger and more empowered than ever.

So, why is it imperative to discern between internal and external challenges? Because awareness lays the groundwork for effective problem-solving and personal evolution. By pinpointing the origins of our obstacles, we gain insight into our strengths and weaknesses, empowering us to devise targeted strategies for surmounting adversity.

Reflective Question: What internal and external challenges have peppered your journey, and how have they shaped your resilience and determination moving forward?

Action Steps:

1. Embrace self-reflection to identify and understand your internal obstacles.
2. Develop targeted strategies to tackle both internal and external challenges head-on.
3. Cultivate a supportive network to provide guidance and encouragement during times of adversity.

So, let's embrace the profound impact of both internal and external challenges, recognizing their role in shaping our journey towards growth and resilience.

4.3. Learning to Bounce Back from Setbacks

Ever felt like life just sucker-punched you when you least expected it? You're cruising along, thinking you've got it all figured out, and then BAM! Life throws you a curveball that knocks you off your feet. But hey, here's the thing: setbacks are just detours, not dead ends.

Take the story of Jamie, a young entrepreneur with big dreams. She poured her heart and soul into launching her startup, believing she was on the brink of success. But then, just as things were gaining momentum, the market took a nosedive, and her business went belly up. Jamie was crushed, feeling like she'd hit rock bottom.

But instead of wallowing in self-pity, Jamie decided to turn her setback into a setup for a comeback. She dusted herself off, learned from her mistakes, and pivoted her business model. It wasn't easy, and there were plenty of late nights fueled by coffee and sheer determination. But Jamie refused to let failure define her. She embraced the challenge, seeing it as an opportunity to grow and evolve.

And you know what? Jamie's resilience paid off. Not only did she rebuild her business from the ground up, but she also emerged stronger and more resilient than ever before. She learned that setbacks are just part of the journey, not the destination. They're the fuel that ignites our determination and propels us forward, even when the road ahead seems uncertain.

So, how do you bounce back from setbacks like a boss? It starts with embracing failure as a teacher, not a tormentor. Stop dwelling on what went wrong, instead redirect your attention and focus and learn the valuable lessons from the experience. Every setback is an opportunity to course-correct and come back stronger than before.

Reflective Question: Think about a time when you faced a major setback. How did you bounce back from it, and what lessons did you learn in the process?

Action Steps:

1. Don't be afraid to fail, mate! Taking a tumble can help you climb higher in the end. If somethin' doesn't go as planned, don't sweat it. Instead, use that as a chance to learn and become a better version of yourself.
2. Surround yourself with a support system of friends, family, and mentors who can lift you up when you're feeling down.
3. Practice resilience-building exercises like mindfulness, gratitude, and self-care to strengthen your mental and emotional resilience.

Remember, setbacks are not the end of the road; they're just a temporary detour. When it comes to achieving your goals, setbacks are inevitable. But don't let them discourage you. Keep pushing forward, and remember that each setback is actually a step closer to your ultimate success.

Keep bouncing back, my friend. You've got this!

4.4. Developing Coping Strategies for Managing Stress and Uncertainty

Ever felt like life's a never-ending game of dodgeball, and you're the only player without a helmet? 🏐 💥 Are you sick and tired of feeling like life is throwing curveballs at you left, right, and center? Me too! Stress and uncertainty seem to be the bane of our existence, but I've got news for you: it doesn't have to be that way. Developing effective coping strategies can help you overcome obstacles and come out the other side stronger than ever.

Let me tell you about my friend Mike. He was going through a pretty rough patch in life, dealing with a bad breakup, a job he hated, and personal health issues. But instead of wallowing in self-pity, he decided to take control of the situation. He started exercising, eating healthier, and taking steps to find a more fulfilling job. He even started volunteering at a local shelter, which gave him a sense of purpose and fulfillment. Through this experience, Mike learned that obstacles can be turned into opportunities for growth if you're willing to put in the work.

So, how can you develop coping strategies for managing stress and uncertainty? First and foremost, you need to take responsibility for your own well-being. Instead of waiting for things to magically get better, take action and start making changes in your life. Whether it's setting boundaries with toxic people, seeking therapy, or pursuing a new hobby, you have the power to make positive changes in your life.

Another key aspect of coping with stress and uncertainty is to reframe your mindset. Instead of seeing challenges as something to be feared, view them as opportunities for growth. When you encounter an obstacle, ask yourself questions like, "What lessons can I learn from this?" or "How can I use this experience to become a better version of myself."

Now, Listen up, folks, let me ask you, what changes can you make in your life to take responsibility for your own well-being? A version of myself?"

How can you reframe your mindset to view challenges as opportunities for growth? Finally, don't be afraid to seek support when you need it.

Whether it's confiding in a trusted friend, engaging in a support group, or seeking professional help, there is no shame in asking for support. In fact, it's a sign of strength to recognize when you need help and take action to get it.

Reflective question

Think back to a time when life threw you a curveball. How did you initially respond, and what coping strategies did you employ to navigate through the uncertainty? Who can you turn to for support when you need it?

Action Steps:

1. Take Inventory of your coping Toolbox. What strategies have worked for you in the past, and how can you enhance or expand upon them?

2. Prioritize Self-care. Whether it's carving out time for hobbies, exercise, or relaxation, make self-care a non-negotiable part of your routine.
3. Seek Support. Don't hesitate to turn to friends, family, or professional resources for guidance and encouragement during challenging times.

Obstacles are bound to come our way in the game of life, yet they need not dictate our destiny. By taking responsibility for your own well-being, with resilience, self-awareness, and a dash of humor, reframing your mindset, and seeking support when you need it, we can navigate through challenges and emerge even stronger. So, why wait? Seize the moment, take action, and embark on the path to a brighter, more fulfilling future today!

Remember, you're not just dodging dodgeballs—you're mastering the art of the game. Keep playing, keep growing, and keep shining! ❇

4.5. Seeking Meaning and Growth in the Face of Difficulties

Ever feel like life's treating you like a punching bag, relentlessly throwing blows from all directions? Are you buried under an avalanche of obstacles, struggling to catch your breath? And in those darkest moments, have you questioned the very reason for your existence? It's tough, I know. But let me introduce you to Jade—a true warrior on the battlefield of life. Despite facing trials that would break the strongest spirits, she survived and thrived. Her story is one of resilience, of triumph over adversity, and it's nothing short of inspiring.

Jade's journey resembled a turbulent rollercoaster, plunging into depths of despair and soaring to heights of hope. She was always a go-getter, harboring grand dreams of making a difference in the world. However, when the devastating news of her diagnosis of a rare autoimmune disease shattered her world, her dreams crumbled like a house of cards. The dreams she had nurtured for so long seemed like distant stars in a cloudy sky. Everything changed. Suddenly, tasks once simple became Herculean feats, and her aspirations appeared unreachable.

At first, Jade felt rushed. She felt like life had kicked her in the teeth, and she didn't know how to get back up again. But Jade wasn't one to stay down for long. Despite the pain and uncertainty, she refused to let her illness define her. With each passing day, Jade found a new purpose in her struggles. She started adjusting to her new reality and realized something important: that she could still make a difference. She began volunteering at a local hospital, where she would spend time with patients who were going through similar struggles. Volunteering at the hospital became her sanctuary, where she could channel her pain into something meaningful.

Sitting beside patients, holding their hands, and listening to their stories, Jade discovered the profound impact of simple gestures. Amid life's challenges, Jade learned that even when life throws you a curveball, you can still find purpose and empathy, realizing her struggles granted her a unique perspective to make a difference. Despite her own suffering, Jade felt connected and found light even in the darkest moments, not just for herself but for others as well.

Instead of giving up on her dreams, she found a new way to pursue them—and in doing so, she discovered a strength and resilience she never knew she had. Through her acts of kindness and compassion, Jade discovered a reservoir of strength within herself that she never knew existed. It is a strength born not from physical prowess but from the depth of her heart and the power of her spirit. And in that realization, she found a renewed sense of purpose and a determination to live her life to the fullest, no matter what obstacles lay in her path.

So, what can we learn from Jade's story? Here are a few takeaways: When life knocks you down, it's easy to feel defeated. But sometimes, the best way to get back up is to focus on helping others.

By shifting your focus outward, you might discover a fresh outlook on your own challenges. It's common to get absorbed in our own issues and lose sight of the broader context. But when we step back and look at the world around us, we may find that there are countless opportunities to make a positive impact—even in the face of adversity. Growth and meaning can come from unexpected places. Sometimes, the things that challenge us the most are the things that ultimately make us stronger and more resilient.

So, if you feel like life is beating the nonsense out of you, take a page from Jade›s book. Look for ways you can help others who may be facing similar struggles. Connect with your values and passions. And remember that even when things seem hopeless, there's always a way forward. You got this.

Now, let's take another real-life incident. Let me introduce you to Jack, a devoted father and husband. When his wife was diagnosed with a serious illness, Jack felt like his world was crumbling around him. But in the depths of despair, he discovered a reservoir of strength he never knew he had. Instead of retreating, Jack became a pillar of support for his family, finding meaning in the act of caring for his loved ones during their darkest hour.

Life's difficulties can leave us feeling lost and disconnected, but within every challenge lies the potential for growth and transformation.

It's during these moments of adversity that we have the opportunity to explore deep within ourselves, uncovering hidden reserves of resilience and courage. By reframing our perspective and seeking meaning in the face of difficulty, we can emerge from life's trials stronger and more enlightened than ever before.

Reflective Question: Take a moment to reflect on a difficult experience you›ve faced. How did you find meaning and growth in the midst of adversity, and how can you carry those lessons forward on your journey?

Action Steps:

1. Embrace gratitude as a daily practice, focusing on the blessings and lessons that each challenge brings.

2. Cultivate self-awareness through introspection and reflection, allowing yourself to uncover profound insights about your purpose and values.
3. Cut yourself some slack, and extend that kindness to others too. We're all on our own journeys through life's highs and lows.

Life's hurdles can feel like sucker punches sometimes, but they're not roadblocks; they're stepping stones to greatness! So when life tosses challenges your way, grab 'em by the horns and turn 'em into opportunities for growth. Your journey may be tough, but with a hefty dose of determination and resilience, you'll conquer every obstacle and emerge stronger than ever! Remember, when life throws its best curveballs, you've got what it takes to knock 'em out of the park! Keep pushing forward because you've already conquered so much. You can do it—you've made it this far, folks!

Embracing Failure as a Learning Opportunity and Stepping Stone to Success

Failure isn't the opposite of success; it's more like the GPS recalculating your route.

Ever tripped and faceplanted, meaning to say fallen flat on your face, only to realize that the ground beneath you is the perfect foundation for your next leap? Embracing failure as a chance to learn is the secret sauce to growth and triumph.

Let's face it—failure stings. It's like taking a shot of vinegar when you expect Coffee. But guess what? That vinegar kick can wake you up faster than any caffeine jolt.

Take Samantha, for example. She dove headfirst into her startup dream, only to see it nosedive. Instead of licking her wounds, she strapped on her boots and started hiking. Failure became her boot camp, toughening her up and teaching her things no success ever could.

But let's keep it real—embracing failure doesn't mean slapping on rose-colored glasses and pretending it's all sunshine and rainbows. It's about taking the bruises in stride, learning hard lessons, and using them to fuel your comeback.

For Samantha, failure was her boot camp for greatness. It forced her to think sharp, switch gears, and bounce back harder than ever.

Alright, let's dive into Joseph's tale first, and then we'll seamlessly weave in Lily's story.

You know Joseph, right? Or do you remember him from those tales of biblical adventures? Let's journey back to ancient times, where dreams were as real as the stars in the sky; but this time, let's sprinkle a little modern-day flair into the mix.

Picture Joseph, the eleventh son of Jacob, a young dreamer with big aspirations. He had this knack for interpreting dreams, making him quite the favorite of his father, Jacob.

But his older brothers? Well, they weren't exactly thrilled about that.

Now, jealousy? Oh boy, it's like a snake in the grass, coiled and waiting to strike when you're least prepared, lurking silently until the perfect moment to deliver its venomous bite,

Fueled by envy, Joseph's brothers hatched a sinister plot to rid themselves of him. And just like that, Joseph's world comes crashing down when he's betrayed by those closest to him and sold into slavery in Egypt. It's like a sucker punch to the gut, leaving him bruised and broken. And just when you think things couldn't get any worse, Joseph finds himself behind bars in an Egyptian prison, facing a future filled with uncertainty and despair, a far cry from the dreams he once had.

But wait, it gets even more dramatic. Picture Joseph in an Egyptian prison, his future as uncertain as the shifting sands of the desert. It's like a Hollywood movie, with twists and turns at every corner.

Now, fast forward to today's world, where envy and betrayal aren't just relics of the past but daily struggles we all face. Enter Lily, a young professional navigating the cutthroat world of corporate. She's climbing the ladder of success, her ambitions soaring as high as Joseph's dreams once did.

But here's where the plot thickens; Lily's success doesn't sit well with some of her colleagues. They watch with envy as she excels, plotting behind her back like Joseph's brothers did all those centuries ago. And then, just like that, Lily finds herself out of a job, her dreams shattered by the very people she once called colleagues.

But here's the kicker: Like Joseph, Lily refuses to be defeated by adversity. Instead of wallowing in despair, she dusts herself off and sets out on a new path. With determination blazing in her heart and a glimmer of faith lighting her way, Lily embarks on a journey of resilience and self-discovery.

Through the ups and downs, the setbacks and victories, Lily stays true to herself, just like Joseph did all those centuries ago. And you know what?

In the end, her perseverance pays off. She finds success in places she never imagined, and her journey is a testament to the power of resilience and faith in the face of adversity.

Listen then people, how do you turn failure into your best wingman? It's about seeing it as a pit stop, not the final destination. It's about dusting yourself off, grabbing the lessons, and sprinting forward, fueled by the fire of newfound wisdom.

Now, you know how to turn failure into your secret weapon, don't you? Head up—it starts with rewiring your brain—seeing failure not as a dead end but as an alternative route leading to better things. It's about mining gold from every faceplant, no matter how knotted, and using it to slingshot yourself towards your dreams. Flipping the script allows you to turn setbacks into setups for your greatest victories.

So, if you're facing your own trials and tribulations, take a page from Joseph and Lily's playbook. Embrace the challenges, trust in your inner strength, and let their stories inspire you to overcome whatever life throws your way. Remember, if Joseph and Lily can do it, so can you.

Reflective Question

Think back to a moment when you stumbled and fell flat on your face. What lessons did you extract from that tumble? How did you bounce back from that setback, and what pearls of wisdom did you pick up along the way? And how did they propel you forward on your journey?

How does the story of Joseph inspire you to overcome your own challenges?

Action Steps:

1. Embrace that growth mindset like a boss, knowing that failure isn't a reflection of your worth but a chance to level up.
2. Don't be afraid to ask for feedback and soak up constructive criticism like a sponge. It's the secret sauce to refining your skills and strategies.
3. Time to flex that resilience muscle and bounce back from failure stronger than ever! You've got what it takes to conquer any challenge that comes your way, so keep pushing forward with unwavering determination.

Remember, in the game of life, failure isn't a red card; it's your chance to score big. So, lace up those boots, dust off those shoulders, and strut forward with the swagger of someone who knows that setbacks are just setups for epic comebacks.

Keep hustling, keep learning, and keep slaying because failure? It's not the end of the game; it's the beginning of your championship season!

4.7. Cultivating Emotional Intelligence to Navigate Through Challenges

Ever felt like your emotions are running the show, turning your life into a rollercoaster ride of highs and lows? Well, buckle up because it's time to take control of the emotional whirlwind and steer towards smoother waters. Let's kick things off with a little bit of storytime.

Alright, folks, gather 'round for a tale as old as time—well, maybe not that old, but definitely as epic as they come. Picture this: in the ancient land of Israel, there lived a young shepherd named David. Now, David had a knack for slinging stones and strumming his harp, but little did he know he was about to face his greatest challenge yet—dealing with the green-eyed monster named Saul. (The green-eyed monster is traditionally used to describe jealousy, but Saul's specific eye color isn't mentioned in historical texts. It's more of a colorful expression to convey his envy towards David's success.)

Saul, the king of Israel, wasn't too pleased with David's rise to fame. He saw David's popularity soaring higher than his own chariots and decided he didn't like it one bit. Cue the envy, folks! Saul's jealousy reached epic proportions, and he set out to squash David like a bug.

But here's where things get interesting—instead of succumbing to the drama, David kept his cool. He didn't let Saul's bitterness get under his skin. Nope, not our David. He stayed composed, focused on his goals, and even played soothing tunes on his harp to calm Saul's troubled soul. Talk about emotional intelligence in action!

Now, let's bring David's tale into the modern era. Picture yourself slipping into David's sandals, facing down your own Saul—whether it's a—whether it's a jealous coworker, a frenemy's antics, or even that little voice whispering doubts in your head. But fear not, my friend, for like David, you've got the power to keep your cool amidst the chaos.

So, how do we tap into that inner David and conquer life's unexpected hurdles? It's all about self-awareness—tuning in to our thoughts, feelings, and bodily cues. Once we've got that down, we're equipped to hit the brakes when our emotions threaten to spiral out of control and threaten to run wild. Just as David maintained his cool, and held his ground in the face of Saul's jealousy; we, too, can learn to keep our cool when faced with adversity.

Now, fast forward to today, where we've got our own modern-day heroes. Take Mother Teresa, for instance. Born into poverty, she faced unimaginable hardships, yet her unwavering compassion and emotional strength propelled her to become a beacon of hope for millions.

But let's get real for a moment. We're not all saints or kings but believe me, we do have the power to cultivate emotional intelligence and steer through life's storms like champs. It's not just about knowing how you feel; it's about mastering those emotions and using them as fuel for growth. With every obstacle we overcome, we're one step closer to finding peace amid life's storms.

Alright then, let's dive into the art of sharpening our emotional superpowers! It all begins with self-awareness—that knack for tuning in to our thoughts, feelings, and bodily sensations. Once we've got a handle on ourselves, navigating life's rollercoaster becomes a whole lot smoother. So, buckle up and get ready to ride sensibly with clarity and purpose!

But wait, there's more. We've also got to learn the art of self-regulation—the ability to hit the brakes when our emotions threaten to take the wheel and run wild. Just like David remained composed in the face of Saul's jealousy, we, too, can learn to keep our cool when faced with adversity.

Reflective Question

Now, let's sprinkle in some reflective questions to stir the pot.

Think back to a time when your emotions got the better of you. Recall a recent challenge where emotional intelligence played a role in your response. How did it influence your actions?

How could a deeper understanding of your feelings have changed the outcome? And what's one step you'll take to nurture emotional intelligence moving forward?

Last but not least, there are **Action Steps**:

1. Embrace the challenges, trust in your inner strength, and let the stories of David and Mother Teresa inspire you to conquer whatever life throws your way.
2. Think about those moments when your emotions threatened to hijack your rationality—heated arguments, heart-pounding confrontations, adrenaline-fueled decisions. Now, picture hitting the pause button, taking a deep breath, and responding with serene clarity. That's the magic of emotional intelligence in action.

"Listen up, folks! If David and Mother Teresa could waltz through their struggles with faith, we sure can, too. So, buckle up; it's time to welcome the challenges, embrace the chaos, tap into our inner fortitude, and move forward with grit. Together, we'll tackle the peaks and valleys, armed with the mighty force of emotional intelligence. Let's pledge to transform every setback into a springboard to magnificence!"

Tag line:

Emotional intelligence: the ultimate armor against life's curveballs—sharpen your wit, not just your sword, because even your feelings deserve a strategy.

4.8. Building a Support System to Provide Encouragement and Assistance

Have you ever felt like you're scaling Mount Everest solo? Trust me, I've been there and done that.

Life's journey throws us curveballs that can feel like massive mountains to conquer. But here's the kicker: You don't have to brave it alone. It's about rallying your own squad of Sherpas—your support system—to navigate through life's most rugged terrain. Think of it as curating your personal dream team—a crew of allies primed to root for you, lend a hand when you stumble, and hoist you up when you triumph.

In the complex web of life, we're all threads woven together, each with our own unique role to play. Picture a bustling colony of ants diligently gathering sustenance for their community. Each ant knows its role, driven by an instinctual purpose. Then there are the bees, fluttering around their queen bee, devotedly working to safeguard her, aware that their combined efforts ensure the hive's survival.

Now, imagine yourself as one of these tiny creatures navigating the complexities of life. Just like the ants and bees rely on each other for survival, we, too, rely on our support systems to flourish. Whether it's friends lifting us in times of despair, family offering unwavering love, or mentors guiding our path, each member of our support network plays a pivotal role in our journey.

Let me tell you a story that illustrates the power of a support system:

Meet Enid, a young professional navigating the tumultuous waters of her career. Despite her best efforts, she often found herself overwhelmed and doubting her abilities. It was during one particularly challenging project that Enid realized the importance of her support system.

As deadlines loomed and stress mounted, Enid's mentor, Sharon, stepped in with words of encouragement and practical advice. Sharon's unwavering belief in Enid's abilities gave her the confidence to push through obstacles and deliver her best work.

But Sharon wasn't the only one who provided support. Enid's colleagues rallied around her, offering assistance and camaraderie when she needed it most. Together, they formed a tight-knit team that tackled challenges head-on and celebrated victories together.

Through the ups and downs of her career, Enid leaned on her support system time and again. Their encouragement and assistance acted as a safety net, allowing her to take risks and pursue her goals with confidence.

Here, we see how Enid's story highlights the transformative power of a support system. It's a reminder that we don't have to navigate life's challenges alone. With the right people by our side, we can overcome obstacles, achieve our dreams, and find strength in the face of adversity.

Why is having a support system crucial? Let's break it down. Just as every organ keeps the body ticking, our support network keeps us thriving. It's our lifeline, fueling us with strength and resilience in tough times. Whether it's a pep talk, a helping hand, or a listening ear, our support system keeps us focused and grounded. As ants and bees depend on each other, we rely on our support network to navigate life's challenges.

Now, how do you build this powerhouse of support? Recognize: no one's an island. Every member, like cogs in a machine, keeps you on track. They offer shoulders to lean on, sounding boards for ideas, and voices of reason. Imagine trekking a mountain path alone versus with a safety net of champions cheering you on.

But here's the kicker: it's not just about warm bodies. It's about deep connections with those who uplift and understand you. Let's unite and create our ideal support systems, embracing friends, family, mentors, and online communities. Together, we can conquer the world.

And the most important support? It's you. Offer yourself self-compassion, celebrate wins, and know asking for help is okay.

Reflective Question

Take a moment to reflect on your current support system. Who are the individuals who uplift and encourage you? How can you nurture these relationships and deepen your connections in the days ahead?

Reflect on a time when you leaned on your support system. How did their encouragement and assistance impact your journey?

Action Steps:

1. Cultivate meaningful connections: Reach out to friends, family, or mentors who uplift and inspire you.

2. Be a support for others: Be first to accept than to be accepted.
3. Offer encouragement and assistance to those in need, fostering a reciprocal relationship.
4. Prioritize Self-care: Take time to recharge and nurture yourself, recognizing that self-support is crucial in building a strong foundation.

So, let's weave this support system with threads of compassion, strength, and understanding, knowing that together, we can weather any storm.

4.9. Practicing Self-Compassion and Forgiveness During Tough Times

Ever found yourself trudging through a swamp of self-doubt and regret, each step heavier than the last? It's in these moments of darkness that embracing self-compassion and forgiveness emerges as more than just a lifeline—it becomes a guiding light leading us back to shore.

Imagine this: You've made a mistake—a big one. The weight of it sits heavy on your shoulders, threatening to drown you in a sea of shame and guilt. But instead of criticizing yourself for your shortcomings, what if you extended a hand of kindness and understanding? What if you allowed yourself the grace to learn and grow from your mistakes? C'mon now don't be ruthless with yourself.

Picture this: Angela, a diligent professional, makes a critical error at work that risks a major project. Consumed by self-doubt and fear of reprimand, she spirals into a cycle of harsh self-criticism. However, with the gentle encouragement of a supportive colleague and a moment of introspection, Angela learns to forgive herself, recognizing that mistakes are opportunities for growth rather than reasons for condemnation.

In life's journey, we're bound to stumble and fall, often leaving us bruised and battered. Yet, it's our response to these setbacks that truly defines our character. By practicing self-compassion, we offer ourselves the same kindness and empathy we readily extend to others, allowing us to navigate turbulent waters with resilience and grace.

Remember that time when you tripped over your own feet in front of your crush? Or the time you accidentally sent a text meant for your best friend to your boss instead? Life's blunders are inevitable, but by embracing self-compassion, we can laugh at our mishaps and learn from them, rather than allowing them to weigh us down with regret.

So, why is self-compassion essential? Because it serves as a shield against the arrows of self-doubt and criticism, allowing us to face adversity with courage and kindness. And how do we cultivate self-compassion? By acknowledging our humanity, embracing our imperfections, and extending the same forgiveness to ourselves that we would offer to a friend in need.

In practicing self-compassion, we not only heal our own wounds but also create space for growth and resilience. It's a journey of self-discovery and acceptance, one that leads us towards greater empathy, understanding, and ultimately, inner peace.

Reflective Question: How can you incorporate self-compassion and forgiveness into your daily life, especially during challenging times?

Action Steps:

1. Embrace your humanity and imperfections, practicing self-compassion daily.
2. Forgive yourself for mistakes, viewing them as opportunities for growth.
3. Foster a nurturing inner dialogue, offering kindness and empathy to yourself in tough times. Learn from those who exemplify self-compassion, drawing inspiration from their journeys.
4. Just like you wouldn›t skip brushing your teeth or checking your phone, make self-care an essential part of your daily routine. It›s more than just pampering yourself with bubble baths and scented candles (though those are delightful too). Self-care means nourishing every aspect of your being—body, mind, and spirit. So, whether it's starting your day with meditation, taking a refreshing walk in nature, or indulging in your favorite hobby, prioritize activities that recharge your batteries and uplift your soul. And always remember, self-care isn't selfish; it's a wise investment in your overall well-being that yields rich dividends in all aspects of your life.

In the grand journey of life, self-compassion and forgiveness serve as our guiding stars through the darkest nights. By extending grace to ourselves, we unlock the door to resilience and growth. Remember, my fellow travelers, self-compassion isn't just a virtue—it's the cornerstone of our humanity, leading us towards greater empathy, understanding, and inner peace. So, let's embark on this journey together, embracing our imperfections and forging ahead with courage and kindness.

4.10. Celebrating Victories and Milestones Along the Journey of Overcoming Challenges

Ever found yourself standing at the summit of a personal triumph, the wind tousling your hair, the crisp air filling your lungs as you gaze out at the vast landscape of your achievements? This moment of triumph didn't come easy; isn't it? it's the culmination of countless steps taken, obstacles overcome, and victories celebrated along the way. It's moments like these that make the trials and tribulations of life's challenges all worth it. Let's take a moment to bask in the glory of our victories and reflect on the milestones we've reached along the way.

Picture this: You've just conquered a seemingly insurmountable obstacle, whether it's acing a difficult exam, landing your dream job, or overcoming a personal struggle. In that moment of triumph, you're filled with an overwhelming sense of pride and accomplishment. It's a feeling like no other, a reminder of just how resilient and capable you truly are.

But celebrating victories isn't just about patting ourselves on the back and moving on to the next challenge. It's about taking the time to savor the moment, to acknowledge the hard work and dedication that went into achieving our goals. It's about recognizing the progress we've made and the growth we've undergone along the way.

And let's not forget the importance of marking milestones along the journey. Whether it's reaching a certain milestone in your career, hitting a fitness goal, or achieving a personal milestone, each step forward deserves to be celebrated. These milestones serve as markers of our progress, reminding us of how far we've come and motivating us to keep pushing forward.

But perhaps the most important aspect of celebrating victories and milestones is the opportunity it provides for reflection and gratitude. It's a chance to look back on the challenges we've overcome, the lessons we've learned, and the people who have supported us along the way. It's a chance to express gratitude for the opportunities we've been given and the blessings we've received.

But why is a celebration so crucial in the face of adversity? Because amidst life's challenges, it's easy to get bogged down by negativity and self-doubt. By celebrating our victories, no matter how small, we reaffirm our belief in ourselves and our ability to overcome obstacles. It's a reminder that we are capable of greatness, even in the midst of adversity.

And let's not forget the power of celebration to fuel further progress. When we acknowledge and celebrate our achievements, we're more motivated to continue pushing forward, even when the going gets tough. It's like adding fuel to the fire of determination, propelling us ever closer to our goals.

So, how can we celebrate our victories and milestones effectively? It's all about finding what works for you. Whether it's treating yourself to a small indulgence, sharing your success with loved ones, or simply taking a moment to bask in the glow of accomplishment, find ways to acknowledge and honor your achievements.

So, as we celebrate our victories and milestones, let's not lose sight of the lessons learned along the way. let's take a moment to reflect on the journey that has brought us to this point. Each victory and milestone is an opportunity for growth and reflection. Let's express gratitude for the challenges that have shaped us, the setbacks that have made us stronger, and the victories that have filled us with joy. Reflect on how far you've come and use that momentum to propel you forward on your journey.

And let's carry that sense of gratitude and celebration forward as we continue to navigate the challenges that lie ahead.

As we close the chapter on navigating challenges, remember that celebration is not just about the destination; it's about embracing the journey with all its ups and downs. So, take a moment to raise a toast to yourself and all that you've accomplished. You've earned it.

With this celebration, we bid farewell to Chapter 4, ready to embark on the next leg of our journey with renewed strength and determination.

Reflective Question: How do you approach challenges in your life?

Action steps:

1. **Reflect on Challenges:** Take a moment to reflect on the challenges you've faced recently. Consider what you've learned from these experiences and how they've helped you grow.
2. **Celebrate Victories:** Identify a recent achievement, no matter how small, and celebrate it. This could involve treating yourself to something you enjoy, sharing your success with friends or family, or simply taking a moment to acknowledge your accomplishment.
3. **Set Future Milestones:** Look ahead and set some achievable milestones for yourself. It's beneficial to divide big goals into smaller, achievable steps and to plan how to celebrate each milestone once it's reached. This approach is an effective way to maintain motivation and keep track of my progress.

CHAPTER 5

FULFILLMENT UNLEASHED: BALANCING PASSION AND REALITY

*H*old on tight as we dive into the rollercoaster ride of self-discovery and fulfillment! In this chapter, we'll unravel the fascinating interplay between passion and reality exploring how they intersect to create a life of true contentment.

Let's go!

5.1. Exploring the Concept of Fulfilment and Its Components

Ever pondered the elusive nature of fulfillment? It's a journey into the heart of what truly matters, a quest to uncover the essence of a deeply satisfying life.

Picture this: You're standing at the crossroads of your existence, grappling with the age-old question of what it means to lead a fulfilling life. It's a question that beckons exploration, inviting you to dive into the depths of your desires and aspirations.

Let me share a story with you. Meet Ancy, a corporate executive who seemingly has it all—a high-paying job, a fancy car, and a luxurious penthouse. Yet, despite her outward success, Ancy yearns for something more that money can't buy. Despite the accolades and achievements, a nagging sense of dissatisfaction lingered like a stubborn shadow. Through a series of soul-searching adventures and profound revelations, Ancy embarks on a quest to unravel the true meaning of fulfillment.

Fulfillment isn't just about chasing fleeting pleasures or material possessions. It's about aligning your actions with your values, cultivating meaningful relationships, and pursuing passions that ignite your soul. It's about living authentically and purposefully, unapologetically embracing who you are and what brings you joy.

Ancy's journey evokes a sense of longing, a universal desire to uncover the secret sauce of fulfillment. It's a journey marked by highs and lows, victories and setbacks, but ultimately driven by the quest for meaning and purpose.

Why does this matter? Because a life without fulfillment is like a ship without a rudder, drifting aimlessly amidst the vast ocean of existence. By understanding the components of fulfillment, you can chart a course that leads to greater satisfaction, purpose, and contentment.

Ever notice how we sometimes chase after external markers of success in pursuit of fulfillment, only to realize that true happiness comes from within? It's like searching for the perfect avocado—sometimes elusive, but oh so satisfying when you find it.

Fulfillment isn't a destination; it's a journey, a dynamic interplay of passion and realism. It's about aligning your actions with your values, pursuing meaningful goals, and finding joy in the process.

As we explore deeper into the concept of fulfillment, it's natural to experience a whirlwind of emotions—from moments of clarity and joy to periods of doubt and introspection. Embrace these emotions as signposts on your journey, guiding you towards a life that resonates with your deepest desires.

Here's a radical idea: What if fulfillment isn't a destination but rather a way of being? This notion challenges conventional wisdom and invites us to redefine success on our own terms. By embracing this mindset shift, you open yourself up to a world of possibilities and opportunities for growth.

So, where do we go from here? Start by reflecting on what fulfillment means to you. What activities make you feel most alive? What values do you hold dear? By answering these questions honestly, you'll gain invaluable insights into what truly fulfills you.

As we embark on this exploration of fulfillment, remember that with each step forward, you're inching closer to a life rich in meaning, purpose, and fulfillment.

Reflective Question: So, as you reflect on your own quest for fulfillment, what components do you believe are essential for a truly satisfying life? How can you strike a balance between following your passions and being realistic in your pursuits?

What does fulfillment look like in your life? Are there any areas where you feel out of alignment with your true desires? Take some time to reflect on these questions and consider how you can cultivate greater fulfillment in your daily life.

To unlock the door to fulfillment, consider practical strategies

Action Steps:

You got it:
1. Reflect on Your Values: Dive deep to uncover what truly matters, what brings joy, fulfillment, and purpose to your life. Understanding your values aligns your actions with your true desires.
2. Chop your goals into bite-sized bits and keep score of your progress. Each small win fuels the drive towards your dreams.
3. Cultivate Gratitude: Daily practice acknowledging blessings, big and small. Appreciate the people, experiences, and opportunities enriching your journey. Embrace gratitude, shifting your focus to life's brighter hues, nurturing fulfillment and contentment within.

With these action steps, you'll be well on your way to unlocking the door to fulfillment and living a life that reflects your true desires and values.

5.2. Identifying Personal Passions and Interests That Ignite Fulfillment

Have you ever found yourself sitting in a bustling café, surrounded by the aroma of freshly brewed coffee, pondering life's greatest mysteries? You're not alone.

Meet Mike, an IT professional who has been working in the industry for over a decade. He's always been good at what he does and well-respected in his field, but something has been gnawing at him for a while now. Despite his success, he feels like something is missing. He's been pondering what that could be for a while now, but he's never been able to put his finger on it.

One day, Mike decided to take a break from his usual routine and attend a local coding workshop. As he worked alongside other programmers, he found himself feeling more energized, excited, and fulfilled than he had in a long time. He realized that what he loved most about his job was the creative problem-solving aspect of it. That was it—the missing piece he had been searching for!

Driven by this newfound insight, Mike started exploring his passion for creative problem-solving. He began attending more workshops, joining online communities, and collaborating with other IT professionals on exciting new projects. With each new experience, Mike felt a profound sense of purpose wash over him like a gentle wave.

But that's not where the story ends. Mike discovered a deep-seated love for teaching others the art of creative problem-solving through his newfound passion. He started mentoring younger programmers, organizing coding boot camps, and even starting his own coding school. It was a calling that resonated with him on a level, igniting a passion he never knew existed.

As Mike explored his newfound passion deeper, he realized that fulfillment wasn't just a destination but a journey. It was about aligning his actions with his innermost desires and crafting an authentic life. Armed with courage and conviction, Mike set out to chart his own course towards a life of purpose and meaning, all while continuing to work in the IT industry that he loves.

Reflective Question: What are you waiting for? Seriously, could you take a moment and think about it? What's keeping you from pursuing your passions and living a more fulfilling life? Is it fear? Laziness? Lack of direction? Whatever it is, it's time to face it head-on and start taking action.

Action Steps:
1. Cut the excuses and figure out what you really want out of life.
2. Break your goals down into small, manageable steps and start taking action.

3. Accept that failure is a necessary part of the process and keep pushing forward.
4. Surround yourself with people who support and encourage you.

The destination isn't everything, buddy. The journey itself is just as crucial, so don't forget to relish the ride.

5.3. Evaluating Practical Considerations and Realistic Constraints

Ever found yourself caught between the allure of your dreams and the harsh realities of daily life? Welcome to the common ground we all tread upon. In this segment, we dive deep into the pragmatic waters, exploring how to navigate the maze of practical considerations and realistic constraints on our journey towards fulfillment.

Life isn't always a smooth sail on serene waters. We face bills to pay, responsibilities to uphold, and obligations to meet. Yet, amidst these challenges lies the question: do we need to relinquish our dreams entirely? Not necessarily.

The crux lies in discerning practical considerations and constraints with a keen eye. While it might seem improbable to abandon everything and pursue a passion like underwater basket weaving full-time, there are ways to integrate it meaningfully into our lives.

So, how do we tread this delicate tightrope between passion and reality? It begins with being brutally honest about our situations and ourselves and candidly assessing our circumstances.

Let me tell you about a real-life incident that perfectly illustrates the importance of evaluating practical considerations. A few years ago, John was a freelance writer who landed a job writing for a major magazine. He was thrilled, but there was one small problem: the deadline was only two days away.

Now, he could have panicked and pulled an all-nighter to get the job done. But instead, he took a step back and evaluated the practical considerations and realistic constraints. He realized that it simply wasn't feasible to write a quality article in such a short amount of time. So, he did something that's not always easy for us Type-A overachievers: he asked for an extension.

To his surprise, the editor was understanding and granted him an extra week to complete the article. And you know what? It turned out to be one of the best pieces he has ever written. If he had charged ahead without evaluating the practical considerations, he would have turned in a subpar article that could have damaged his reputation. Instead, he took a step back, evaluated his options, and made the best decision for himself and his career.

Now, I know this might not seem like the most exciting story in the world, but stick with me. The point is, sometimes, we get so caught up in the "hustle" and the "grind" that we forget to take a step back and think about what's really feasible and realistic. We think we can do it all, but the truth is, we're only human. And that's okay.

Now, Meet Doris—she had a strong passion for photography but was always swamped with her demanding corporate job. One day, she stumbled upon a photography workshop happening nearby in her city and decided to take the plunge. The workshop turned out to be a transformative experience for Doris. She felt a sense of belonging with like-minded individuals who shared her passion, and under the guidance of experienced photographers, her skills grew. With newfound zeal, Doris started integrating photography into her daily life and found creative ways to pursue her passion while balancing her practical responsibilities. In doing so, she discovered a more profound sense of fulfillment and purpose.

So, hey folks, Reflect on what truly holds significance for you and the sacrifices you're willing to make to pursue your dreams. Can you leverage your passions to carve opportunities within your existing limitations? Are there creative solutions to circumvent practical barriers?

While it's crucial to acknowledge the hurdles ahead, it's equally important not to let fear or self-doubt paralyze us. Often, the most profound growth emerges when we step beyond our comfort zones and embrace uncertainty.

Dear reader, remember that passion and reality need not exist in isolation. By evaluating practical considerations and realistic constraints with an open mind and a resilient spirit, we can chart a path towards a life that seamlessly intertwines fulfillment and pragmatism.

Alright, here are some **Reflective Questions** and **Action Steps** for you to consider:

1. What are some practical considerations and realistic constraints in your own life or work that you need to evaluate?
2. What are some areas where you might be pushing yourself too hard, and how can you adjust your expectations to be more realistic?
3. What fears or doubts hinder your pursuit of your dreams, and how can you address them? What are some small steps you can take to prioritize self-care and avoid burnout?

Remember, evaluating practical considerations isn't about giving up on your goals or settling for mediocrity. It's about being honest with yourself about what's genuinely feasible and making the best decisions for your own well-being and success.

Action Steps:

1. Compile a list of your passions and interests.
2. Identify any practical considerations or constraints that might impede your pursuit of these passions.
3. Brainstorm innovative solutions to navigate around these limitations.
4. Take a small, tangible step towards integrating your passion into your daily routine, no matter how modest.

5.4. Crafting a Roadmap for Success

Are you ready to turn your passions into a roadmap for success? Buckle up because, in this section, we're diving headfirst into the exhilarating journey of crafting a plan to pursue your dreams. But first, let me ask you this: Ever felt like you're wandering aimlessly through life, unsure of where you're headed or how to get there? Well, you're not alone. Many of us have dreams and aspirations, but without a clear roadmap, we often find ourselves stuck in neutral.

Enter Alex, a young aspiring writer with a head full of ideas and a heart whole of ambition. For years, Alex had dreamt of penning a novel that would captivate readers and leave a lasting impact. But amidst the hustle and bustle of daily life, the dream seemed to drift further and further out of reach.

One day, while sipping coffee at a local bookstore, Alex had a moment of clarity. It was time to stop merely dreaming and start taking tangible steps towards turning that dream into reality. Armed with a newfound sense of determination, Alex set out to craft a roadmap for success.

Step one? Define the destination. Alex spent hours reflecting on what success would look like as a writer. Was it landing a publishing deal? Seeing their book on display on the shelves of bookstores? Or connecting with readers on a deep emotional level? By clarifying the end goal, Alex gained clarity on the steps needed to get there.

Next up? Break it down. Alex knew that writing a novel was a monumental task, so they broke it down into smaller, more manageable chunks. Setting weekly word count goals, outlining plot points, and scheduling dedicated writing sessions became the cornerstone of Alex's plan.

But crafting a roadmap wasn't just about the destination or the journey but also about flexibility. Life has a funny way of throwing curveballs, and Alex knew that adaptation would be key to staying on course. So, they built in checkpoints and pivot points along the way, allowing for adjustments as needed.

Reflective Questions:

1. What does success look like to you when pursuing your passions?
2. How can you break down your long-term aspirations into smaller, actionable steps?
3. What obstacles or challenges do you anticipate along the way, and how will you overcome them?

Action Steps:

1. Define Your End Goal: Take time to envision what success looks like in pursuing your passions.
2. Break It Down: Identify the smaller, achievable steps needed to reach your ultimate destination.
3. Stay flexible: Build in checkpoints and pivot points to adapt to unexpected challenges and opportunities.

Crafting a roadmap for success is like embarking on an epic adventure filled with unforeseen obstacles and hurdles that compel you to grow and evolve. It's more than just reaching your destination; it's about enjoying the adventure along the way. To make it happen, you need to identify your passions, break them down into small, actionable steps, and remain adaptable in the face of challenges. Armed with these tools, you'll be able to pursue your dreams with purpose and determination. So, let's start mapping out your path to success and witness as you turn your aspirations into reality!

5.5. Time Management Techniques

Alright, let's dive into the realm of time management. Now, I know what you're thinking—time management sounds about as exciting as watching paint dry. But trust me, my friend, mastering the art of time management is like unlocking the secret to a more fulfilling and balanced life.

Meet Eden, a passionate graphic designer juggling a full-time job, freelance projects, and a budding art career. Sound familiar? Eden found herself constantly struggling to find time for her creative pursuits amidst the chaos of her daily responsibilities. But instead of throwing in the towel, Eden decided to take control of her schedule and make every minute count.

Step one? Identify the time sucks. Eden realized she was spending too much time mindlessly scrolling through social media and binge-watching Netflix after work. So, she made a conscious effort to limit her screen time and reclaim those precious hours for her passion projects.

Next up? Prioritize ruthlessly. With a million things vying for her attention, Eden knew she had to be ruthless about where she allocated her time. She identified her top priorities—her art career and freelance projects—and made sure to carve out dedicated blocks of time for them each week.

But effective time management isn't just about saying no to distractions—it's also about saying yes to self-care. Eden learned the hard way that burning the candle at both ends only leads to burnout. So, she made sure to schedule regular breaks, exercise sessions, and downtime to recharge her batteries.

Reflective Questions:

- How do you currently spend your time, and are there any areas where you could be more efficient?
- What are your top priorities in life, and how can you ensure they get the attention they deserve?
- How do you feel when you're overwhelmed with tasks and responsibilities, and what strategies can you implement to alleviate that feeling?

Action Steps:

1. Audit Your Time: Track how you spend your time for a week and identify any areas where you could be more intentional.
2. Prioritize Your Passions: Determine what matters most to you and make sure to allocate time for those activities each day or week.
3. Schedule Self-care: Remember to prioritize your well-being. Schedule regular breaks, exercise sessions, and downtime to recharge your batteries.

Time management isn't about squeezing every last minute out of the day—it's about making intentional choices that align with your values and priorities. By identifying your time sucks, prioritizing ruthlessly, and scheduling self-care, you'll be well on your way to creating a life that's both productive and fulfilling. So, let's take control of our schedules and make every moment count on the journey to pursuing our passions.

5.6. Overcoming Procrastination

Alright, moving on, let's tackle the age-old rival of productivity: procrastination. Tell me, have you ever found yourself putting off important tasks only to feel overwhelmed and guilty later on? If so, you're not alone. Procrastination has a sneaky way of creeping into our lives and sabotaging our best-laid plans.

Meet Jason, a passionate film maker with big dreams of launching his first short film novel. Sounds exciting, right? But here's the catch—Jason has been stuck in a cycle of procrastination for months, unable to muster the motivation to sit down and shoot. Sound familiar? Despite his burning desire to share his creativity and real life stories through movies with the world, Jason finds himself endlessly scrolling through social media, binge-watching Netflix, and finding any excuse to avoid the shooting of his short film .

So, how does Jason break free from the grips of procrastination and reclaim his creative spark? It all starts with a shift in mindset. Instead of viewing procrastination as a character flaw, Jason learns to see it as a natural response to fear and uncertainty. By acknowledging his fears and embracing vulnerability, Jason gains the courage to confront his procrastination tendencies head-on.

But overcoming procrastination isn't just about mindset—it's also about setting yourself up for success. Jason creates a dedicated editing space free from distractions, establishes a daily filming routine, and breaks his daunting goal of making a film into smaller, more manageable tasks. With each small victory, Jason builds momentum and gains confidence in his ability to overcome procrastination.

Reflective Questions:

- What fears or uncertainties are driving your procrastination tendencies, and how can you address them?
- How do you feel when you procrastinate, and what strategies can you implement to break free from this cycle?
- What tiny, doable actions can you take right now to kick procrastination out of your life and start making headway towards your goals?

Action Steps:

1. Identify your triggers: Pay attention to the situations or emotions that trigger your procrastination tendencies.
2. To achieve your goals, break big projects into smaller, manageable tasks. This avoids feeling overwhelmed and provides a clear roadmap for progress. Remember, taking the first step is key!

3. Alright, let's get real here. If you're serious about achieving your goals, you need to create an environment that supports your success. That means setting up a workspace that's free from distractions and establishing a daily routine that keeps you focused and motivated. Trust me, it's worth the effort. With the right environment and routine in place, you'll be unstoppable. So get to it!

Look, procrastination is a sneaky enemy. It creeps up on us when we least expect it, distracting us from the important tasks at hand and lulling us into a false sense of security. But don't be fooled—with the right approach, we can kick procrastination from our lives and unleash our true potential. It all starts with cultivating the right mindset and implementing effective strategies to stay on track. So, let's get to it and show procrastination who's the boss!

5.7. Setting Healthy Boundaries with Others

Have you ever felt like you're constantly being pulled in a million different directions by the demands of others? Tell me, have you ever found yourself saying yes to everyone else's needs while neglecting your own? It's a common predicament, my friend, but fear not—we're diving deep into the art of setting healthy boundaries with those around us.

Let me introduce you to David, a people-pleaser extraordinaire who can't seem to say no to anyone. Whether it's staying late at the office to help a colleague or sacrificing his weekend plans to attend yet another family gathering,

David's calendar is always packed with obligations to others. Sound familiar? Despite his best intentions, David's inability to set boundaries leaves him feeling drained and overwhelmed, with little time or energy left for himself.

But here's the kicker—David eventually reaches a breaking point. After yet another week of overcommitting and underdelivering, he realizes that something's gotta give. It's time to take a stand and reclaim control over his time and energy.

So, how does David learn to set healthy boundaries with others without feeling guilty or selfish? It all starts with a shift in mindset. Instead of viewing boundaries as barriers to connection, David learns to see them as essential tools for maintaining his well-being and preserving his sanity.

But here's the kicker—David doesn't stop at just recognizing the importance of boundaries. He takes proactive steps to communicate his needs and limits clearly and assertively, whether it's with his demanding boss, his needy friends, or his overbearing relatives. And you know what? The world doesn't end—in fact, it's quite the opposite. By setting healthy boundaries, David finds that he's able to show up more fully and authentically in his relationships, fostering deeper connections and greater respect from those around him.

Reflective Questions:

- What areas of your life are currently lacking in healthy boundaries, and how is it affecting your well-being?

- What fears or beliefs are holding you back from setting boundaries with others, and how can you overcome them?
- What specific boundaries do you need to establish in order to prioritize your own needs and goals?

Action Steps:

1. Identify Your Priorities: Take some time to reflect on what matters most to you in life, and identify the areas where you need to set boundaries to protect those priorities.
2. Practice Assertiveness: Start small by assertively communicating your needs and limits in low-stakes situations, gradually building your confidence to set boundaries in more challenging circumstances.
3. Set Clear Boundaries: Establish clear and specific boundaries with others and communicate them openly and respectfully. Remember, setting boundaries isn't about being selfish—it's about taking care of yourself so you can be your best self in all areas of life.

Hey there! I›ve got a great tip for you today: learning to say «No» can really simplify your life and make you feel more in control. So many of us struggle with saying «No» to others, whether it›s our boss, friends, or family members. But it›s important to remember that your time and energy are valuable, and you have the right to prioritize them as you see fit.

That's why I encourage you to master the art of saying "No" with confidence and grace. It may take some practice, but once you get the hang of it, you'll feel much more empowered and in charge of your life. So next time you're faced with a request that doesn't align with your goals or values, don't be afraid to decline politely.

Remember, saying "No" doesn't make you a bad person—it just means you're setting healthy boundaries and taking care of yourself. And that's something to be proud of!

Yo, listen up! Suppose you want to maintain your well-being, preserve your sense of self, and not lose your mind dealing with other people's gibberish. In that case, you gotta learn how to set healthy boundaries. Recognize your own needs and limits, and communicate them like a boss.

When you prioritize authentic connections built on mutual respect and understanding, you can avoid the toxic trap of simply tolerating everyone's nonsense and save yourself from just putting up with everyone's crap.

5.8. Leveraging Technology and Resources

Now listen up , do you ever feel like you're drowning in a sea of information and technology, struggling to stay afloat amid the constant barrage of emails, notifications, and social media updates? Have you ever wondered how to harness the power of technology and available resources to support your passions and goals?

Meet Cathy, a passionate artist with dreams of turning her creative hobby into a full-fledged career. But here's the thing—Cathy is overwhelmed by the sheer amount of information and tools available to her. From online courses and tutorials to social media platforms and networking groups, the possibilities seem endless. Sound familiar?

But fear not, dear reader, for Cathy soon discovers the magic of leveraging technology and resources to streamline her pursuit of passion. Instead of feeling overwhelmed by the abundance of options, she learns to embrace them as valuable tools for her journey.

So, how does Cathy make technology work for her rather than against her? It all starts with intentionality and focus. She sets clear goals for herself and identifies the specific resources and tools that will help her achieve them. Whether it's signing up for an online course to refine her skills or joining a community of like-minded artists for support and inspiration, Cathy takes deliberate steps to leverage technology in service of her passions.

But here's the kicker—Cathy doesn't stop at just consuming information and resources. She takes action. She applies what she learns, seeks feedback from mentors and peers, and uses technology to showcase her work and connect with potential clients and collaborators. In doing so, she not only accelerates her progress but also expands her network and opportunities for growth.

Reflective Questions:

1. How are you currently leveraging technology and resources to support your passions and goals?
2. What specific tools or platforms could you explore to streamline your workflow and enhance your productivity?

3. Can you strike a balance between using technology as a tool for growth and avoiding its pitfalls, such as distraction and information overload?

Action Steps:

Assess Your Current Resources: Take stock of the technology and resources available, and identify any gaps or areas for improvement.

Set Clear Goals: Define specific, measurable goals for yourself, and determine how technology can help you achieve them.

- Don't just consume information passively—take action on what you learn.
- Experiment with new tools and strategies.
- Seek feedback to refine your approach.

In today's digital age, technology offers a wealth of opportunities to support our passions and goals. By leveraging the power of technology and available resources with intentionality and focus, we can streamline our workflow, expand our network, and accelerate our progress towards living a life aligned with our deepest desires. So, here's to embracing technology as a valuable tool on our journey of growth and self-discovery—may we use it wisely and purposefully to unlock our full potential.

5.9. Reflecting on the Journey of Balancing Passion and Pragmatism

Have you ever found yourself in a sticky situation in life where you are at a crossroads between following your heart and being practical? Let's face it, this can be a tough call to make. You may have often pondered how to strike the right balance between chasing your dreams and handling the nitty-gritty of day-to-day existence. But fear not, my friend. It's a common predicament, and I'm here to help you navigate through this dilemma. Let's dive in and find a way to steer you towards both fulfillment and practicality, shall we?

Let me introduce you to Jimmy, a dreamer with his head in the clouds and his feet firmly planted on the ground. John has big aspirations—to travel the world, start his own business, and live life on his own terms. But there's a catch—John also has bills to pay, a family to support, and responsibilities that demand his attention. Sound familiar?

But here's the thing about Jimmy—he refuses to settle for a life of mediocrity. Instead of succumbing to the pressures of practicality, he embarks on a journey to find harmony between his passions and pragmatism. And let me tell you, it's no easy feat.

Along the way, Jimmy encounters obstacles and setbacks that threaten to derail his dreams. There are bills to pay, deadlines to meet, and expectations to fulfill. But with each challenge, Jimmy learns valuable lessons about resilience, adaptability, and the power of perseverance.

Reflective Questions:

1. How do you currently balance your passions with practical considerations in your own life?

2. What challenges have you faced in pursuing your dreams, and how have you overcome them?
3. Are there areas where you feel out of alignment with your true desires, and if so, what steps can you take to course-correct?

Action Steps:

Reconnect with your passions:

1. Listen up, my friend. Stop chasing what other people think will make you happy and start focusing on what truly lights you up.
2. Take a moment to reflect on what brings you joy and fulfillment in life.
3. Once you've identified those things, make them a priority and align your activities accordingly.
4. Don't waste your time on things that don't matter to you.

Life is too short to live someone else's dream.

Assess your practical considerations: Identify any external factors or responsibilities that may impact your ability to pursue your passions, and develop strategies to work around them.

Take intentional action:

- Set clear goals for yourself.
- Break them down into manageable steps.
- Take consistent action towards realizing your dreams.

In the journey of balancing passion and pragmatism, there are bound to be ups and downs, twists and turns. But by staying true to ourselves, embracing challenges as opportunities for growth, and taking intentional action towards our dreams, we can navigate this delicate dance with grace and determination. So, here's to reflecting on our journey thus far, learning from our experiences, and charting a course towards a life filled with purpose, passion, and fulfillment.

CHAPTER 6

BREAKING NORMS: REDEFINING FULFILLMENT ON YOUR OWN TERMS

*A*lright, buckle up, folks! It's time for Chapter 6, —where things really start to heat up."It's time to buckle up and brace yourself for an exhilarating journey as we plunge headlong into the nitty-gritty of this thing called life.

Now, I know what you're thinking. "Oh great, another self-help book telling me what to do with my life." But let me tell you something: this is different from your average book. This is a book that's going to make you sit up and take notice. "Yo, listen up! Life isn't gonna just fall into your lap! It's gonna give you a good smack and say 'Wake up, buddy!'" So, let's get down to business.

In this chapter, we're going to talk about the importance of taking risks. That's right, I said it. Risks. Because let's face it, if you want to live a life that's truly worth living, you'll have to take a few calculated risks along the way. Now, I'm not talking about skydiving or bungee jumping (although those are definitely risks worth taking if that's your thing). I'm talking about taking risks in your career, relationships, and personal growth. It's about stepping outside of your comfort zone and doing something that scares you. Because when you do that, that's when you truly grow as a person. But I know, I know, taking risks is scary. It's easier to just stay in your little bubble and not rock the boat.

But let me tell you something, my friend. If you never take risks, you'll never know what you're truly capable of. You'll never know what amazing things you could accomplish if you just dared to go for it.

So, let's make a deal. Let's make a pact to take more risks in our lives. Let's promise each other that we'll push ourselves out of our comfort zones and take on something that leaves us feeling uneasy but, ultimately, fulfilling. Because when we do that, that's when we truly start living.

So if you're ready to challenge the norms, flip the bird to convention, and carve out your own path to happiness, then let's do this thing! It's time to break free from the shackles of society and embrace the exhilarating journey of living life on your own terms!

Dare to defy the status quo. You live only once. It's your life. Do it right!

6.1. The Evolution of Norms: How Society Defines What is "Normal"

It's fascinating to observe how societal norms have changed over time. What was once considered taboo or deviant is now accepted as normal. For example, interracial marriages were once frowned upon, but now they're widely accepted. Society's evolving perspectives on issues like gender, sexuality, and race have reshaped our understanding of what's "normal." But what exactly are norms? Have you ever thought about the unwritten rules that govern our behavior? These rules, also known as norms, can significantly impact our lives. Norms are the unsaid rules that govern our behavior. They're the unspoken expectations that we follow to fit into society. Norms can be anything from how we dress, to how we talk, to how we behave in social situations.

Look, let's get real here. While we've made some progress on breaking down outdated norms, there's still a lot of crap out there that's doing more harm than good. Take beauty standards, for example. The pressure to conform to a certain look can seriously mess with our heads, leading to all kinds of nasty body image issues and low self-esteem. And don't even get me started on gender norms. These archaic ideas about what men and women should be doing can seriously limit our potential and choices. Let's all agree to ditch these toxic norms and start living our lives on our own terms, yeah?

But it's important to remember that norms are not set in stone. They're not immutable laws that we must follow blindly. We have the power to challenge and redefine what's considered "normal." By doing so, we can create a more inclusive, accepting society that allows us to be our authentic selves.

Let me tell you a story about Hannah, my friend. Hannah has always been passionate about expressing herself through her clothing. She loves wearing bold colors, mixing patterns, and taking risks with her fashion choices. But growing up, Hannah was often teased and ridiculed for her clothing choices. Her classmates called her "weird" and "out of touch."

Hannah's experience is a perfect example of how societal norms can be limiting and oppressive. For a long time, she felt like she had to conform to what was considered "normal" in order to fit in. But as she got older, Hannah realized that she didn't want to hide her true self anymore. She wanted to embrace her unique style and express herself authentically.

So Hannah started experimenting with her wardrobe again. She began wearing the clothes that made her feel confident and happy, regardless of what others thought. And you know what? People started to take notice. Hannah's bold fashion choices became a conversation starter, and she found that people were drawn to her for her authentic self-expression.

Hannah's story is a powerful reminder that we don't have to conform to societal norms in order to be accepted. We can embrace our unique identities and challenge what's considered "normal." By doing so, we can create a world that celebrates diversity and individuality.

Reflective Questions:

1. What societal norms have you personally challenged or broken?
2. How have these experiences impacted your sense of self?
3. What are some societal norms that you believe need to be challenged or changed?

Action Steps:

1. Identify a norm that you would like to challenge or break. Start by taking small steps towards that goal.
2. Surround yourself with people who support and encourage you to be your authentic self.

Let me give it a shot: As we navigate society's ever-changing landscape, our understanding of what is considered "normal" is bound to transform. By challenging and redefining these norms, we can cultivate a more inclusive and compassionate world that celebrates the richness of human diversity and individuality.

6.2. Shattering Conventions: Embracing Your Unique Identity

Hey there, folks! Are you feeling like you're the odd one out? Like nobody around you gets you, and you're constantly suppressing parts of yourself just to fit in? Yeah, that's a pretty common feeling, and it can leave us feeling pretty isolated and misunderstood. But what if I told you that embracing your unique identity is the key to living a fulfilling and authentic life?

I recently met a girl named Alexa, who had always felt like an outsider. She had a thing for punk rock music and loved skateboarding, but her conservative family didn't understand her interests. So, she tried to conform to their expectations for years, but it just left her feeling empty and unfulfilled. It wasn't until she embraced her love for punk rock and skateboarding that she finally felt like she was living authentically.

Alexa's story is a reminder that breaking free from the norm can be scary, but it's also incredibly liberating. When we give ourselves permission to be who we truly are, we open ourselves up to a world of possibilities. We no longer feel the need to conform to societal norms or the expectations of others. Instead, we can focus on living a life that is true to ourselves.

But let's be honest: embracing your unique identity isn't always a walk in the park. It can be tempting to suppress our authentic selves just to fit in or avoid judgment. But here's the thing: those who judge us for being different are not worth our time or energy. Life's too short to waste it on people who don't accept us for who we are, quirks and all.

Now, I know what you might be thinking—why should I embrace my unique identity? Well, I've got a little secret for you: authenticity is magnetic. When you fully embrace who you are, quirks, and all, you start to attract people and opportunities that align with your true self. So, don't be afraid to stand out from the crowd and let your uniqueness shine bright. Whether you're into '80s hair bands or collecting antique teapots, embrace what makes you different. Your quirks are what make you—you, and they should be celebrated, not suppressed.

Listen up, people. It's time to stop giving heed to what others think and start embracing your weirdness. Seriously, the world needs more authentic individuals who are unapologetically themselves. Don't suppress your quirks, passions, or interests just to fit in with society's expectations. Instead, embrace them as a part of who you are and let your freak flag fly high. Trust me, living a fulfilling and authentic life starts with accepting your unique identity.

"Hey there, buddy! You're a one-of-a-kind masterpiece of the creator, born with your own unique qualities that make you truly exceptional. Don't you agree that you deserve recognition for your special talents and abilities?"

Reflective Questions:

1. What aspects of your identity do you feel most hesitant to embrace?
2. How can you cultivate more self-acceptance and confidence in expressing your true self?
3. What steps can you take today to honor your authenticity and live life on your own terms?

Action Steps:

1. Embrace your quirks: Instead of hiding your unique traits, celebrate them as badges of honor that make you who you are.

2. You know what's important? Surround yourself with folks who understand and champion your authenticity. So, take action—seek out your tribe. Those kindred spirits who journey with you, lifting you higher and guiding you towards your best self. They see your potential, cheer your wins, and weather storms by your side. In life's symphony, they're the uplifting notes, lighting your path. Treasure these allies, for they're life's true gems, enriching your self-discovery journey.
3. Take small steps outside your comfort zone to express your true self in various aspects of your life, whether it's through your fashion choices, hobbies, or career decisions.

Look, my friend, embracing your unique identity isn't just an act of rebellion; it's a powerful declaration of self-love and empowerment. So, don't you dare slouch, stand tall and proud of who you are, and let your authenticity light up the world.

6.3. Exploring Personal Values and Authentic Desires

Ever felt like you're playing a role in someone else's movie instead of starring in your own? Like you're following a script written by society, rather than listening to the whispers of your own heart? Let's dive deep into the maze of personal values and authentic desires, and discover what truly sets your soul on fire.

Meet Allan, a high-powered executive who seemed to have it all—the corner office, the fancy car, the designer suits. But beneath the facade of success, Allan felt a gnawing sense of emptiness and disconnection from his true self. Despite his outward achievements, there was a persistent ache for something more, something deeper.

It wasn't until Allan embarked on a journey of self-discovery that he began to unravel the layers of societal conditioning and unearth the treasures buried within his own soul. Through introspection and reflection, he identified his core values—integrity, compassion, and creativity—and realized that these were the guiding principles he wanted to live by.

But Allan didn't stop there. He also dived into his authentic desires—those deep-seated longings that reflected his true essence and purpose.

He discovered a passion for mentoring others and a love for the arts, both of which had been buried beneath the demands of his corporate career.

With newfound clarity and conviction, Allan began to realign his life with his values and desires. He made space for creativity by taking up painting classes and volunteering at a local youth center. He found fulfillment in mentoring young professionals and guiding them on their own paths to success.

Reflective Questions:

- What are your core values, and how do they influence your decisions and actions?
- What are your authentic desires, and how can you incorporate them into your daily life?

- In what ways can you align your actions with your values and desires to live a more authentic and fulfilling life?

Action Steps:

- Take time to reflect on your core values and identufy what truly matters to you.
- Explore your authentic desires—those deep-seated longings that reflect your true essence and purpose.
- Experiment with different activities and experiences to align your life more closely with your values and desires.

By exploring our personal values and authentic desires, we're peeling back the layers of societal conditioning and rediscovering the essence of who we truly are. So, let's embrace the journey of self-discovery and reclaim our authenticity, one step at a time.

6.4. Overcoming Societal Expectations and Pressures

Well, have you ever felt like you're constantly swimming against the current of societal expectations and pressures, like you're living in a fishbowl? It's like we're all trapped in a never-ending game of "keeping up with the competition," where the rules are constantly changing, and the stakes are impossibly high.

Well, well, well, let me tell you a story about societal expectations and pressures. As we all know, growing up, we're surrounded by them. Parents, teachers, peers, and the media—they all tell us the same thing: what we should be doing, thinking, and feeling. But what happens when those expectations clash with our true selves?

I remember when I was in college, I was supposed to follow a certain career path that would lead me to financial stability and success. But deep down, I knew that wasn't what I wanted. I had a passion for writing, but I was too scared to pursue it because it didn't fit the mold of what was deemed as a "successful" career.

Look, I'm not gonna lie—it was tough. It took me a while to summon the courage to pursue writing full-time, but I knew that I couldn't ignore my passion any longer. And you know what? It's the best decision I ever made. I'm living a life that aligns with my values and passion, and it's the most fulfilling thing I've ever experienced.

So, how do we overcome societal expectations and pressures? It's not easy, but it's doable. Firstly, we need to figure out what our true values and passions are. And trust me, that's not always easy. It requires some deep introspection and reflection. But once we have a clear understanding of what we truly want, we can start taking small steps towards that direction.

But hey, let's be honest. It's not all rainbows and unicorns. There will be obstacles and challenges along the way, but that's part of the journey. The important thing is to keep pushing forward and not give up on our dreams.

So, my friend, what do you truly want out of life? What's stopping you from pursuing your passions? Think about it and take action towards your dreams. Remember, life is short—don't waste it living up to someone else's expectations.

Let's have a heart-to-heart about societal expectations and pressures. Undeniably, they can be overwhelming and often prevent us from pursuing our true selves. So, how can we overcome them? Let's start by reflecting on our own experiences.

Reflective Questions:

1. What societal expectations and pressures have you experienced in your life? How have they impacted your decisions and actions?
2. Have you ever felt like you were living a life not aligned with your true self? If so, what steps have you taken to change that?

Action Steps:
1. Take the time to identify your true values and passions. It can be a difficult process, but it's important to reflect on what makes you happy, what you're naturally good at, and what you want to achieve in life.
2. Once you've identified your true self, start taking small steps towards it. You can start pursuing a new hobby or passion or making minor changes to your daily routine that align with your values.

Remember, the journey won't be easy. You will face obstacles and challenges along the way, but don't give up on your dreams. Surround yourself with a supportive community of people who share your values and passions and will encourage you to pursue your true self.

In conclusion, forget about societal expectations and pressures. Break free from the chains holding you back. Reclaim your autonomy and authenticity. Live life on your own terms. Rewrite the rules and embrace the beauty of a fulfilling existence.

6.5. Embracing Unconventional Paths and Choices

Do you feel stuck in life, unsure which path to take? Or unsure of what choices to make? Do you find yourself torn between tradition's well-worn path and the unconventional's uncharted territory? I know the feeling all too well. It's a familiar dilemma for many, myself included.

But let me tell you a little story about someone who dared to take the road less traveled and found fulfillment in the most unexpected places.

Gideon, a humble farmer in an era of oppression, was an unlikely hero. He was timid and unsure of himself. But when God called him to lead an army against the enemy, he rose to the occasion, displaying courage and leadership that were unconventional for someone like him.

When Gideon was called upon to lead an army against the enemy, he came up with an unconventional plan. Instead of gathering a large army, Gideon gathered just 300 men. Then, he equipped each man with a trumpet and a torch hidden inside a clay jar.

Under the cover of darkness, Gideon and his men surrounded the enemy camp. At Gideon's signal, they blew their trumpets and smashed the jars, revealing the torches inside. The sudden burst of light and noise created confusion among the enemy, who thought a much larger force was attacking them.

In a stunning turn of events, the enemy, amid the chaos, turned on each other. Gideon's small army emerged victorious without even drawing their swords. This was a triumph that defied all expectations, a testament to the power of unconventional thinking and creative problem-solving. It seemed like a crazy plan, but it worked. They defeated the enemy, and Gideon became a hero.

What can we learn from Gideon's story? Sometimes, the path to success isn't a straight line. By using an unexpected and unconventional strategy, Gideon overcame overwhelming odds and achieved a seemingly impossible victory. His story shows us that sometimes, the path to success isn't a straight line. Sometimes, it's the unconventional paths and choices that lead us to greatness. But why is that?

When we take risks and try something new, we are forced to think creatively and outside the box. We develop resilience and perseverance, and we learn from our failures. We become more adaptable and open-minded. And when we succeed, we gain confidence and a sense of accomplishment that can propel us forward.

Here is Shane, a free spirit who dared to take the road less travelled and found fulfillment in unexpected places.

Shane refused to conform to society's expectations. While his peers were busy chasing money and status, Shane was busy pursuing his passions and charting his own course.

Shane's unconventional path included a variety of activities that were not considered mainstream. For example, he pursued backpacking trips to remote parts of the globe, often venturing off the beaten path to explore new destinations. He also pursued passion projects that defied societal norms, such as creating art that pushed the boundaries of traditional art forms.

In addition, Shane pursued alternative forms of income, such as freelancing and starting his own small business. He was not afraid to take risks and try something new, even if it wasn't the most popular or conventional choice.

At first, Shane's unconventional choices were met with skepticism and concern from friends and family. They questioned why he wasn't following the traditional path to success. But Shane remained undeterred, fueled by a burning desire to forge his own destiny and live life to the fullest. And so, Shane set out on a series of unconventional adventures.

But why did Shane choose to take the road less traveled? It's simple—he wanted to live a life that was true to himself, pursue his passions, and find fulfillment in the things that mattered most to him. Shane knew that the traditional path to success wasn't for him, and he was willing to take risks and try something new to find his own way.

So, what can we learn from Shane's story? Sometimes, unconventional paths and choices lead us to greatness. When we try something new, we develop power and strength that can propel us forward. Shane's story is a testament to the power of embracing unconventional paths and choices. Don't be afraid to chart your own course, pursue your passions, and live life on your own terms. You never know where it might lead you.

Because when we succeed, we gain confidence and a sense of accomplishment that can fuel our future endeavors. Shane encountered challenges and setbacks along the way, but each obstacle only strengthened his resolve to stay true to himself. He learned to think creatively and outside the box, developing resilience and perseverance that would serve him well in all areas of life.

Listen up! I now challenge you to break free from your routine and boldly step towards the unfamiliar tasks. Embrace the unconventional, think outside the box, and make magic happen. Don't be afraid to take risks and push your limits because that's where true growth and fulfillment lie. So, what are you waiting for? Let's dive into uncharted waters and conquer the world!

Reflective question: What unconventional path or choice have you been avoiding? Why have you been avoiding it?

Action Step: Take a step outside your comfort zone and embrace the unconventional. It could be as simple as pursuing a passion project or taking a trip to a new destination.

Alright, just take a minute and ask yourself, what's holding you back from pursuing some unconventional paths and making bold choices in your life? Maybe it's the fear of going after a career that doesn't fall into the typical mold, or taking a trip to an entirely new country, or even starting your own business. Whatever it may be, I urge you to get out of your comfort zone and embrace the unconventional. It might just be the best decision you ever make!

In conclusion, embracing unconventional paths and choices can be scary, but it can also be the key to unlocking your full potential. Take a lesson from Gideon's story and step outside your comfort zone. You never know where it might lead you.

6.6. The Role of Social Media in Challenging Conventions

Hey there, fellow seekers of truth! So, you've found yourself trapped in the endless scroll of social media, bombarded by cat videos and perfectly posed selfies. But are you aware of the hidden depths of this digital realm? What if I told you there's more to this digital playground than meets the eye? Look, my friend, we're about to dive into the deep end of social media and see what kind of crazy stuff we can discover, so be ready for anything. We might just uncover something that could change the way we see the world. Are you game for challenging the norm and finding out what's really going on?

Imagine this: You're mindlessly scrolling through your feed, and suddenly, BAM! You stumble upon a post that hits you like a ton of bricks. It's not your typical meme or viral trend; it's a powerful call to action, challenging societal norms and demanding change. In a world of superficiality, this post stands out like a beacon of hope, reminding us that social media can be a force for good.

"Alright, let's take a step back and consider how we ended up here. Once regarded as a mere playground for self-obsessed and attention-seeking individuals, social media has transformed into a battleground for social justice and activism. With movements like #MeToo and climate change protests gaining momentum, social media has emerged as a potent tool for organizing, mobilizing, and raising awareness.

Listen up, folks. It ain't all doom and gloom with social media. Believe it or not, it's actually given everyday people a chance to be themselves without any filter. People are taking advantage of their digital presence to shatter beauty standards, dismantle stereotypes, and open up about their personal struggles. Whether it's the body positivity movement or mental health awareness, social media is giving a voice to those who've been silenced and shaking up the system.

Yo, listen up! If you want to make a difference and shake things up on social media, you have to be intentional about the content you consume and create. Don't waste your time mindlessly scrolling through your feed. Seek out voices that challenge your perspective and inspire you to think differently. Use your platform to share stories that matter and amplify marginalized voices. That's how we spark meaningful conversations and create a real impact.

But let's not kid ourselves; change won't happen overnight. It requires us to be mindful of our online behavior and its impact on others. So, stop comparing yourself to others and start cultivating a culture of empathy and understanding. Use your likes, shares, and comments to lift others up and create a more inclusive and compassionate online community. That's how we really make a difference!

Now, picture this: it's a typical Tuesday afternoon, and you're scrolling through your social media feed, mindlessly double-tapping on cute puppy pics and drooling over delicious food videos. But amidst the sea of memes and hashtags, something catches your eye—a post challenging the status quo, questioning the norms, and inviting you to think outside the box.

Meet Sera, a regular Jane like you and me, who decided she'd had enough of the same old same old. Tired of seeing cookie-cutter posts and airbrushed perfection, she took a leap of faith and started sharing her raw, unfiltered thoughts with the world. And guess what? People started listening.

With every post, Sera sparked conversations, ignited debates, and inspired others to speak their truth, too. Suddenly, social media wasn't just a mindless distraction—it was a platform for change, a virtual soapbox where ordinary people could challenge conventions and shake up the status quo.

Now, you might be thinking, "But Sera's just one person. What difference can she really make?" Ah, but here's the thing: Sera isn't alone. She's part of a growing movement of truth-seekers, rebels, and dreamers who refuse to be silenced by the noise of conformity.

And that's where you come in. Yes, you! Because, just like Sera, you have the power to challenge conventions and make your voice heard. Whether it's through a thought-provoking post, a captivating story, or a simple act of kindness, you have the ability to spark change and inspire others to join the conversation.

So, the next time you're scrolling through your feed, don't just passively consume content—be the content. Be the voice of reason in a world gone mad, the beacon of hope in a sea of cynicism. And together, let's use social media not just to connect but to challenge, inspire, and change the world, one post at a time.

Because hey, if Sera can do it, so can you. And who knows? Maybe one day, your name will be the one inspiring others to challenge conventions and make a difference in the world.

In conclusion, social media has the power to be a force for good, but it's up to us to make it happen. Let's use our platforms to challenge conventions, spark conversations, and create a more just and equitable world—one post at a time.

Reflective Questions:

1. How can you use your social media platform to challenge conventions and spark meaningful conversations?
2. What topics or issues are you passionate about, and how can you incorporate them into your online presence?
3. In what ways can you support and amplify the voices of others who are challenging conventions and advocating for change on social media?

Action Steps:

1. Start by identifying one convention or norm that you'd like to challenge or question on social media.
2. Craft a post or message that invites your audience to engage with the topic and share their thoughts and experiences.
3. Encourage dialogue and respectful debate by actively responding to comments and engaging with different perspectives.

Listen up, folks. Every single post you make has the power to make a real difference. So don't hold back; let your voice be heard loud and clear. Together, we can shake things up and make a real impact.

6.7. Building Resilience Against Criticism and Judgment

Ever felt like you're living under a magnifying glass, with every move scrutinized and every decision questioned? Welcome to the club! In this section, we will learn how to armor ourselves against the arrows of criticism and judgment, embracing our uniqueness and standing tall in the face of naysayers.

Have you ever been told you're not good enough? Yeah, join the club! But here's the thing—who gets to decide what "good enough" even means?

Imagine this: You're strutting down the street, feeling like the king or queen of the world, when suddenly, someone throws shade your way. Instead of letting it ruin your vibe, you brush it off with a smirk and keep on strutting. That's the kind of resilience we're aiming for, where you're in control of your reactions and empowered by your own self-worth!

Criticism and judgment are like raindrops in a storm—inevitable and sometimes relentless. But just like a sturdy umbrella, we can build resilience to weather the storm and emerge stronger on the other side. By understanding that criticism often says more about the critic than the criticized, we can learn to let it roll off our backs like water off a duck.

Take Cindy, for example. She's a budding artist who faced backlash from her family when she decided to pursue her passion instead of a traditional career. But instead of crumbling under the weight of their judgment, she used it as fuel to propel herself forward, proving them wrong with her success.

Who are we living our lives for—ourselves or others? It's time to break free from the chains of external validation and dance to the beat of our own drum. Remember, your self-worth is not determined by others' opinions, but by your own belief in yourself.

Reflective Question: How can you turn criticism into constructive feedback and use it to fuel your growth rather than hinder it?

Action Step: Practice self-compassion and remind yourself that you are worthy and capable, regardless of what others may say.

6.8. Creating Your Own Metrics for Success and Fulfillment

Do you ever feel like you're stuck in a game with a set of rules that you didn't choose? It's time to break free of the constraints and create your own standards for success and satisfaction. In this section, we'll dive into how you can define success on your own terms, march to your own tune, and evaluate your progress based on what truly counts to you.

Who decided that success meant climbing the corporate ladder or owning a fancy car? Let's rewrite the script and define success on our own terms.

Picture this: You're at a family gathering, and Aunt Mildred asks when you're going to get a "real job." Instead of launching into a defense, you whip out your list of accomplishments—from mastering the art of sourdough bread to finally beating that impossible video game level. Take that, Aunt Mildred!

Society loves to slap labels on success—big house, fancy car, corner office. But true fulfillment comes from aligning your actions with your values and passions, not ticking off someone else's checklist. By creating your own metrics for success, you reclaim your power and pave your own path to happiness.

Meet Tom, a rebel with a cause. Instead of chasing after society's idea of success, he decided to measure his worth by the impact he made on others. From volunteering at soup kitchens to mentoring underprivileged youth, Tom found fulfillment in making a difference, not in his bank account balance.

Success is not a one-size-fits-all equation. It's about defining what success means to you and having the courage to pursue it unapologetically, even if it means colouring outside the lines and thinking out of the Box. Get this: Pizza is round but comes in a square box; thought about it anytime?

Reflective Question: What would your life look like if you measured success based on your own values and passions rather than societal expectations?

Action Step: Take some time to reflect on what truly matters to you and jot down your own metrics for success. Then, commit to living by those metrics, regardless of what others may think.

6.9. Overcoming Fear and Judgment: The Power of Being True to Yourself

Alright, folks, let's cut the chase and get real for a second. We live in a world where the pressure to fit in is about as subtle as a sledgehammer to the face. And let me tell you, trying to be someone you're not is like wearing a scratchy wool sweater in the middle of summer—uncomfortable as ever. But folks, let's navigate the treacherous waters of fear and judgment with the finesse of a ninja on caffeine.

6.9.1. Setting the Stage: Fear and Judgment

Picture this: You're at a party, desperately trying to blend seamlessly into the background like a chameleon that's been hitting the gym a bit too hard. But no matter how hard you try, you can't shake the feeling that you're just not measuring up. Sound familiar? Yeah, we've all been there. Fear has a way of sneaking up on you like a ninja in the night, whispering sweet nothings of self-doubt into your ear.

And don't even get me started on judgment. It's like we're all auditioning for the lead role in a reality TV show, where the panel of judges transforms into armchair psychologists armed with overly critical opinions, all too eager to dismantle anyone daring to stray from the expected, all in a bid to prop up their own fragile egos.

6.9.2. The Art of Not Giving Heed: Embrace Your Inner Weirdo

So, how do you rise above the disharmony of fear and judgment and reclaim your sanity? Simple. Embrace your inner child character like it's going out of style. Authenticity is like a trusty cast iron skillet—it becomes seasoned and more flavorful with each use. So why waste your time trying to be a watered-down version of someone else when you could be a full-bodied, unapologetically awesome version of yourself?

Forget about fitting into society's little boxes and start coloring outside the lines. Wear that Hawaiian shirt to the office on a Monday. Dance like nobody's watching at the grocery store. Embrace your quirks and peculiarities like badges of honor, and watch as the world bows down at your unbridled awesomeness.

6.9.3. Why Bother?

Now, you might be wondering, "Why should I bother with all this authenticity nonsense?" Well, my friend, let me break it down for you. Normalcy is overrated. It's similar to attempting to force a square peg into a circle—and you're likely to wind up feeling frustrated and irritated.

But when you embrace your true self, magic happens. Suddenly, you're not just existing, you're freaking thriving. You're living life on your own terms, flipping the bird to anyone who dares to tell you otherwise. And let me tell you, there's nothing more liberating than saying "Forget you" to societal expectations and forging your own path like a bold trailblazer.

Reflective Question: Take a moment to reflect on the last time you felt the suffocating grip of fear and judgment. How did it make you feel? And more importantly, how can you channel that experience into fuel for your journey towards authenticity?

Action Step: Today, do something that scares the living daylights out of you. Whether its signing up for that stand-up comedy class, you›ve been eyeing or finally telling your Aunt Mildred that her meatloaf sucks, embrace the discomfort like a boss, and watch as your confidence soars to new heights.

In a world that's constantly trying to push you into a neatly labeled box, being true to yourself is the ultimate act of rebellion. So go ahead, unleash your inner self with reckless abandon. Embrace your flaws, quirks, and imperfections like they're the keys to your own personal kingdom. Because, spoiler alert: they are. And trust me when I say the view from the top is spectacular.

6.10. The Journey to Self-Acceptance: Embracing Your Unconventional Path

Alright, folks, buckle up because we're about to embark on a wild ride—the journey to self-acceptance. But here's the kicker: we're not taking the well-trodden path. Oh no, we're blazing our own trail through the untamed wilderness of authenticity.Be there with me!

6.10.1. Navigating the Wilderness: Embracing Unconventionality

Picture this: You're standing at the crossroads of conformity and rebellion, and you choose the road less traveled. You're not here to fit neatly into society's cookie-cutter molds. No, you're here to wholeheartedly embrace your quirks, your peculiarities, your exquisitely unconventional self.

6.10.2. The Art of Radical Acceptance: Embracing Imperfection

So, how do you embark on this journey of self-acceptance? It starts with a radical act of defiance—embracing your imperfections. You see, perfection is overrated. Chasing perfection in the desert is like chasing an illusion—you'll never reach it, and you'll end up parched and exhausted. But when you embrace your flaws and imperfections, you tap into a wellspring of power and resilience.

6.10.3. The Road Less Traveled: Forging Your Own Path

Forget about following in the footsteps of others. This journey is yours and yours alone. It's about forging your own path through the wilderness of life, guided by the compass of your own authenticity. Sure, it might be rocky at times, but the view from the summit is worth every stumble and scrape along the way.

6.10.4. Embracing the Unpredictable: Finding Beauty in Chaos

Life is messy. It's unpredictable. And that's what makes it beautiful. Embrace the chaos, the uncertainty, the glorious unpredictability of it all. Because it's in those moments of chaos that we discover who we truly are—strong, resilient, beautifully flawed human beings.

Reflective Question: Take a moment to reflect on the unconventional aspects of yourself that you've been hesitant to embrace. How can you start honoring and celebrating those parts of yourself today?

Action Step: Today, do one thing that scares you, but also excites you—a small act of rebellion against the status quo. Let your authenticity shine through; whether it's wearing mismatched socks or starting that passion project, you've been putting off.

Conclusion: In a world that's constantly clamoring for conformity, choosing your unconventional path is a bold declaration—an act of self-love that resonates with the very essence of who you are. So, go ahead, cast aside apprehension, and embrace the beauty of your flaws, the richness of your uniqueness. Because ultimately, it's not about blending in—it's about standing out, illuminating the world with the brilliance of your authenticity.

CHAPTER 7

MONEY MATTERS: NAVIGATING FINANCIAL WELLNESS ON YOUR PATH TO PURPOSEFUL LIVING

So, dear readers, you want to live a purposeful life. You've identified your passions, set goals, and are ready to conquer the world. But wait, where does money fit into all of this? Money isn't just about paying bills or buying stuff; it's a tool that can either hinder or propel your journey towards purposeful living.

Money plays an important role in our lives, and it's essential to understand how it fits into our journey towards purposeful living. In this chapter, we'll explore the different ways money impacts our lives and how we can navigate financial wellness on our path to happiness and fulfillment.

7.1 Understanding the Role of Money in Purposeful Living -Understanding How Money Fits Into Your Life

7.1.1. Understanding How Money Fits Into Your Life

Listen up, folks. I'm not here to sugarcoat it, so I'll just say it straight: understanding the role of money in our lives is absolutely crucial. Let me paint you a picture. You're out there, day in and day out, fighting tooth and nail for a cause you believe in—environmental conservation. You've got this dream of starting your own nonprofit to protect endangered species. But here's the deal: without money, that dream of yours ain't going nowhere. It's just going to stay lodged in your brain like a stubborn thought. That's where the greenbacks come in, my friend. Money is what fuels your passion and turns it into action. So, if you're serious about making a difference, you better start getting serious about the role of money in your life.

Money ain't the be-all and end-all; it's just a tool to get what we want. Don't go thinking that money is the ultimate goal, 'cos it ain't. Money can bring us comfort, safety, and freedom, but it won't make us happy on its own. We gotta understand how money fits into our lives so we can use it smartly and not get too caught up in chasing more and more of it.

7.1.2. Overcoming Financial Stress and Anxiety

Just wanted to share with you that financial stress and anxiety can really mess with your life goals. But, no worries! You can totally take control of your finances and develop a positive relationship with money. It's all about managing your finances like a boss, setting realistic financial goals, and not comparing yourself to others. So, listen up, folks! There's some good news for you. By following these simple steps, you can say goodbye to financial anxiety and start living your best life. Trust me, it's time to take control of your finances and start living on your own terms.

7.1.3. Developing a Mindset of Abundance

Hey, listen up, buddy Alright, pal, listen up! The way we think about money is super important because it has a big impact on our financial well-being. If we keep thinking that we don't have enough, we'll only see the things we're missing and the things we don't have. But if we switch to an abundance mindset, we'll be able to see all the opportunities and possibilities that exist. And believe me, having that kind of mindset can make a huge difference in attracting wealth and abundance into our lives. So if you really want to live a purposeful life, it's time to start focusing on abundance, my friend!

7.1.4. Building Wealth and Creating Financial Freedom

Building wealth and creating financial freedom are essential steps. If you want to achieve financial wellness, you gotta start building wealth and creating financial freedom. But let me tell you, it ain't no easy feat! Building wealth takes time, patience, persistence, and discipline. You gotta have a solid financial plan, invest your money wisely, and stay away from unnecessary risks. Remember, slow and steady wins the race!"

7.1.5. Giving Back and Making a Difference

"Yo, listen up! If you really wanna live a life with a purpose, then it's important to give back and make a difference in the world. You gotta put your resources, including your cash, into creating a positive impact on society. Trust me, when you give back, you feel a sense of fulfillment and purpose that no amount of money can ever buy."

7.1.6. Balancing Money and Happiness

Achieving financial wellness doesn't mean sacrificing our happiness. It's essential to find a balance between our financial goals and our happiness and well-being. We need to prioritize our values and passions and use our money to support them.

7.1.7. Embracing Financial Wellness as a Journey

Finally, look, it's absolutely critical that you understand financial wellness is not a one-time destination that you simply arrive at. It's a never-ending journey that requires consistent effort and attention. As you navigate your way through this financial journey, it's important to be patient, persistent, and adaptable towards achieving your goal of purposeful living. Without a doubt, comprehending the role of money in living with purpose is crucial to achieving financial wellness and living a truly fulfilling life. If you can cultivate a healthy relationship with money, focus on building wealth, and give back to others, you'll be able to make the most of your financial journey and lead a life that truly matters.

Reflective Questions Understanding How Money Fits Into Your Life

1. **Assess Your Money's Role**: How does money currently fit into your life? Is it aligned with your values and goals?
2. **Reflect on Past Decisions**: Consider your financial habits. Are there patterns you'd like to change or improve?
3. **Envision Financial Alignment**: Picture how money can support your purposeful living. What steps can you take to ensure it does?

Action Steps Financial Audit:

Review your finances—income, expenses, savings, debt—to gain clarity on your current situation.

1. **Define Values and Goals**: Identify what's important to you and set clear financial objectives accordingly.
2. **Budget and Educate**: Track spending, seek knowledge on financial topics, and consider seeking professional guidance if needed.

7.2. Assessing Financial Goals and Values
7.2.1. Setting Goals and Knowing What You Value

Alright, listen up, folks. Let's talk about getting your financial game plan sorted. Now, I know some of you might be thinking, "Ugh, setting goals and evaluating values? That sounds tedious." But trust me, this is some of the most important work you'll do when it comes to your finances. It's all about aligning your money habits with what truly lights you up. Sound good? Let's dive in.

7.2.2. What: Setting Financial Goals

First things first, let's talk about setting goals - what's your big picture? What are those financial dreams you have bubbling up inside you?

You can't get where you want to go if you don't have a clue where you're headed. So, take a beat to ponder where you want to land financially. It could be stashing away for a down payment, wiping out student loans, or kickstarting that dream business. Whatever floats your boat, scribble it down, get specific, and set those deadlines. Whatever it is, let's get it down on paper and make it real.

7.2.3. Why: Understanding Your Values

Now, let's dig a little deeper as we move on to values. Why are these goals important to you? What values do they represent?

Knowing what you value in life is key to making smart financial decisions. If you don't know what's important to you, you'll have a hard time prioritizing your spending and saving. So, take a step back and think about what matters most. Maybe it's freedom, security, or the ability to give back to others, or it is spending time with family and friends. Traveling the world or pursuing a career you're passionate about? Understanding the "why" behind your goals gives them meaning and keeps you motivated when the going gets tough. Whatever it is, please write it down and keep it in mind as you make financial decisions.

7.2.4. How: Turning Dreams into Reality

Alright, now for the fun part—making it happen! Chunk those big dreams into bite-sized, doable actions. What can you do today, this week, this month to move closer to your dreams? It's all about taking consistent, intentional action towards the life you envision.

Reflective questions:

1. Think back: what financial goals have you aimed for before? Did you reach them? If not, what hurdles did you encounter?
2. Consider: what are your core three values in life? Do your spending and saving practices today align with those values?

Action Steps:

1. Take a moment to jot down your financial goals, making sure they're clear and trackable.
2. Pinpoint your top three values, and consider how you can sync up your finances with what truly matters to you.
3. Give your budget and spending habits a once-over to ensure they're in line with your goals and values. If not, tweak them until they match up.

7.3. Budgeting and Managing Expenses Effectively

Alright, let's tackle the nitty-gritty of budgeting and keeping those expenses in check. It's all about being smart with your money so you can live the life you want without constantly stressing about finances.

Picture this: You've got your eye on a dream vacation, but every time you check your bank account, its a reality check. Sound familiar? Lets change that.

7.3.1. Making a Plan to Spend Wisely

First things first, let's get organized. Sit down and take a good look at your income and expenses. What's coming in, and more importantly, what's going out? Be honest with yourself here—no sweeping those coffee shop visits under the rug.

Now, let's prioritize. What are your needs versus your wants? Sure, that daily latte might bring you joy, but is it worth sacrificing your dream vacation for? Maybe, maybe not. It's all about finding that balance.

Once you've got a clear picture of where your money is going, it's time to make a plan. Set a budget that allows you to cover your essentials while still leaving room for the fun stuff. And stick to it like glue.

Take my friend Bobby, for example. He used to blow his entire paycheck on gadgets and nights out, leaving nothing for emergencies or savings. However, once he started tracking his expenses and creating a budget, he was able to rein in his spending and start working towards his financial goals.

Reflective Questions:

1. What are your current spending habits? Are there any areas where you could cut back or make adjustments?
2. How do your spending habits align with your financial goals and values?

3. What are some strategies you can implement to spend more wisely and stay within your budget?

Action Steps:

1. Keep tabs on your spending over the next month, sorting them into must-haves and nice-to-haves.
2. Craft a down-to-earth budget that puts your must-haves first while leaving room for a little enjoyment.
3. Keep a close eye on your spending, tweaking things as necessary to keep on course to achieving your financial dreams.

In conclusion, budgeting and managing expenses effectively isn't about depriving yourself of the things you love—it's about being intentional with your money so you can live the life you want without constantly stressing about finances. So, take control of your spending, prioritize what truly matters to you, and watch as your financial goals become a reality.

7.4. Investing in Personal and Professional Growth

Alright, Let's talk about putting some skin in the game when it comes to your personal and professional development. It's time to bet on yourself and watch those investments pay off in spades.

7.4.1. Investing in Yourself and Your Future

Imagine this: You've been eyeing up that online course in web development, but life keeps getting in the way. Sound familiar? Let's flip the script.

Investing in yourself isn't just about throwing money at courses—it's about recognizing your value and committing to your growth, both personally and professionally.

Take Monica, for example. Stuck in a job rut, she finally took the plunge and enrolled in a coding boot camp. Fast-forward a year, and she's landed her dream gig as a web developer, doubling her income in the process.

But self-investment isn't just about climbing the career ladder—it's about enriching your life in unexpected ways. Make it a priority to learn a new language, master an instrument, or dive into mindfulness.

Reflective Questions:

1. What growth areas are calling out to you right now, personally or professionally?
2. Picture your future self. What steps can you take today to invest in that vision?
3. What fears or obstacles are holding you back from investing in yourself, and how can you overcome them?

Action Steps:

1. Pinpoint one area of growth you're keen on and explore resources or courses to kickstart your journey.

2. Carve out time each week to invest in yourself, whether it's hitting the books, attending a class, or honing a new skill.
3. Keep tabs on your progress and celebrate your wins along the way. Remember, investing in yourself is a marathon, not a sprint.

In a nutshell, investing in your personal and professional growth is like planting seeds for a future you'll love. So, bet on yourself, take that leap, and watch as you soar to new heights.

7.5. Cultivating a Healthy Relationship with Money – Building a Good Relationship with Money

Alright, let's dive into the world of money and mindset. It's time to reshape your relationship with those green bills and cents and turn it into a partnership that serves you well.

Imagine this: You're constantly stressed about your finances, always worrying about bills and debt. Sound familiar? Let's flip the script.

7.5.1. What: Building a Good Relationship with Money

Let's start with the basics. Building a good relationship with money isn't just about making more of it—it's about changing the way you think and feel about it. It's about shifting from scarcity to abundance, from fear to empowerment. It's about viewing money not just as a source of stress or scarcity but as a tool for creating abundance and fulfillment in your life.

7.5.2. Why: Understanding the Importance

Why bother? Well, your relationship with money impacts every aspect of your life—from your mental well-being to your overall financial stability. By cultivating a healthy relationship with money, you're laying the foundation for a more secure.

7.5.3. How: Practical Steps to Take

So, how do you go about building this healthy relationship? It starts with mindset shifts and practical actions. Practice gratitude, set clear financial boundaries, and prioritize your long-term financial goals. By aligning your thoughts and behaviors with abundance and empowerment, you'll gradually reshape your relationship with money for the better.

Take David, for example. He used to dread checking his bank account, viewing money as a source of stress rather than abundance. But through daily gratitude practices and mindset shifts, he transformed his relationship with money. Now, he sees it as a tool for creating the life he desires—a life filled with purpose, joy, and abundance.

David's journey from financial stress to abundance is a testament to the power of mindset shifts and intentional practices. Initially, David faced anxiety and fear whenever he confronted his financial situation. However, he decided to take proactive steps to change his outlook.

David began incorporating daily gratitude practices into his routine. Each day, he took a moment to reflect on the abundance in his life, no matter how small. This simple act of acknowledging the positives helped him shift his focus away from scarcity and towards gratitude.

Additionally, David worked on changing his mindset surrounding money. Instead of viewing it as a source of stress and limitation, he started seeing it as a tool for creating the life he desired. By reframing his relationship with money, David was able to approach financial decisions with a sense of empowerment and possibility.

Over time, these practices became ingrained in David's daily life. As he continued to cultivate gratitude and adopt a more positive mindset, he noticed significant changes in his relationship with money. He no longer dreaded checking his bank account; instead, he viewed it as a tool for manifesting his dreams and aspirations.

Today, David lives a life filled with purpose, joy, and abundance. By embracing gratitude and shifting his mindset, he has transformed his relationship with money and unlocked a world of possibilities for himself.

Reflective Questions:

1. What beliefs or attitudes do you currently hold about money? How do they impact your financial decisions and behaviors?
2. How would your life change if you viewed money as a tool for abundance and empowerment rather than a source of stress and scarcity?

3. What steps can you take to cultivate a healthier relationship with money, both mentally and practically?

Action Steps:

1. Take time to examine your beliefs and attitudes about money. Are there any negative patterns or limiting beliefs holding you back?
2. Practice gratitude daily by acknowledging the abundance in your life, no matter how small.
3. Set clear boundaries and priorities for your spending, and make conscious choices that align with your financial goals and values.

In wrapping up, nurturing a positive bond with money is crucial for leading a life brimming with abundance and satisfaction. By adjusting your perspective and implementing savvy financial management strategies, you have the power to revolutionize your connection with money and open up endless opportunities.

So, welcome abundance with open arms, cultivate gratitude, and witness your financial prosperity soar.

7.6. Planning for Long-Term Financial Security

Alright, let's explore the world of long-term financial planning. It's time to prepare for a future filled with security and peace of mind.

7.6.1. Why Plan for Long-Term Financial Security?

First off, why bother? Well, planning for the long term is like planting seeds for a bountiful harvest. It's about ensuring that you have the resources and stability to live the life you want, both now and in the future. Whether it's retiring comfortably, buying a home, or supporting your loved ones, long-term financial security gives you the freedom to pursue your dreams without constantly worrying about money.

7.6.2. How to Plan for Long-Term Financial Security

So, how do you go about planning for the long term?

Alright, let's break down how to tackle long-term financial security, shall we? It all begins with setting crystal-clear objectives and sketching out a path to reach them. Pinpoint what matters most to you—be it squirreling away for retirement, establishing an emergency fund, or investing in your kids' education. Then, devise a plan detailing how you'll turn those goals into realities, factoring in your income, expenses, and comfort with risk.

Take Susan, for instance. With a burning desire to retire early and explore the globe, she got down to brass tacks and crafted a meticulous financial blueprint. Starting with maxing out her retirement accounts, dabbling in low-cost index funds, and tightening her belt to save every penny possible, Susan demonstrated remarkable foresight and discipline. And voilà—thanks to her strategic thinking, she bid farewell to the workforce at 50, fulfilling her lifelong dream of jet-setting across the globe.

Now, let's dive into what you can do to follow suit:

Reflective Questions:

1. What dreams do you harbor for your financial future, and why do they hold such significance for you?
2. What hurdles or roadblocks do you envision on the path to achieving these aspirations, and how can you navigate them?
3. How do your current financial behaviors align with your long-term ambitions, and where might you need to tweak your approach?

Action Steps:

1. Outline your long-term financial aspirations, breaking them into bite-sized, actionable chunks.
2. Evaluate your present financial state, pinpointing areas ripe for bolstering savings or wise investments.
3. Draft a comprehensive financial roadmap detailing the strategies you'll employ to realize your objectives. Be sure to review and tweak your plan periodically as circumstances evolve.
4. By rolling up your sleeves and diving into the nitty-gritty of long-term financial planning, you set the stage for a future brimming with stability and fulfillment. So, don't hesitate—start charting your course today, and witness your financial dreams take flight.

Conclusion

In wrapping up, mapping out your long-term financial security is crucial for constructing a future brimming with stability and possibilities. By establishing concrete goals, devising a robust strategy, and staying proactive in handling your finances, you lay down the groundwork for a life overflowing with abundance and contentment. So, don't delay—take that first step today and witness your financial aspirations materialize into tangible achievements.

7.7. Seeking Opportunities for Financial Independence – Finding Ways to Be Independent Financially

Hey there, let's talk about seeking opportunities for financial independence and finding ways to be financially independent. It's time to explore avenues that empower you to stand on your own two feet financially and chart your own course in life. This is a crucial aspect that can help you lead a better life and achieve your goals

7.7.1. Why Seek Financial Independence?

First off, why bother? Well, financial independence isn't just about having a fat bank account—it's about gaining control over your life and choices. It's about breaking free from the shackles of financial dependency and building a future where you call the shots. Whether it's escaping the 9-to-5 grind, pursuing your passion projects, or simply having the freedom to live life on your own terms, financial independence opens up a world of possibilities.

Being financially independent means having enough money to support yourself and your family without relying on others. It gives you the freedom to make your own choices and pursue your dreams without worrying about money.

7.7.2. How to Seek Financial Independence

Alright, let's break down the quest for financial independence, shall we? It begins by spotting chances to broaden your revenue streams and lessen your dependence on external sources. This might entail launching a side hustle, delving into income-generating assets, or embracing frugality to bolster savings. The crucial element? Stay proactive and strategic, always on the lookout for fresh avenues to nurture your wealth and amplify your financial autonomy.

Take Ashley, for example, tired of living paycheck to paycheck, he decided to start a freelance writing business on the side. By leveraging his writing skills and networking with clients, he gradually built up a steady stream of income that provided him with the financial security and flexibility he craved. Today, Ashley enjoys the freedom to work from anywhere in the world and pursue his passions on his own terms—all thanks to his commitment to financial independence.

7.7.2. What to Do: Reflective Questions and Action Steps

So, what steps can you take to pursue opportunities for financial independence? Let's break it down. First off, invest in yourself. This means honing new skills or pursuing further education to boost your earning potential. Next up, consider launching a side hustle or diving into entrepreneurship to bring in extra cash flow.

Moreover, explore avenues to trim your expenses. Whether it's drafting a budget, axing unnecessary costs, or finding clever ways to slash your bills, every penny saved adds up. And don't overlook the power of investments—think stocks, real estate, or other assets that can yield passive income streams.

Finally, develop a robust strategy and establish precise objectives for pursuing financial independence. Maintaining a well-defined roadmap ensures you stay motivated and stay the course towards your envisioned destination.

Reflective Questions: you can ask yourself

1. What does financial independence mean to you, and why is it important?
2. What are my financial goals, and how can I achieve them?
3. What skills or education can I gain to increase my earning potential?
4. - What expenses can I cut or reduce to save money?
5. - What assets or investments can I explore to generate passive income?
6. How can you leverage talents, connections, resources, and networks to create new opportunities for financial independence?

Action Steps:

- Evaluate your current financial standing: Draft a budget plan, keep tabs on your spending, and pinpoint areas for boosting income or trimming expenses.
- Dive into potential side gigs, investments, or entrepreneurial ventures that resonate with your passions and talents—invest in enhancing your skill set or knowledge base.
- Take charge of your financial destiny by diversifying your income sources—explore various investment avenues to steadily lessen reliance on a sole revenue stream.

Conclusion

In wrapping up, venturing into avenues for financial independence is a decisive step towards crafting a life brimming with freedom and contentment. By adopting a proactive, strategic, and resourceful mindset, you can steadily liberate yourself from financial reliance and carve a path towards a future teeming with abundance and potential. So, seize the journey towards financial independence with gusto, and witness as you unveil fresh realms of freedom and empowerment in your journey.

7.8. Overcoming Financial Obstacles and Challenges – Dealing with Problems That Come Up

Alright, let's tackle the inevitable bumps in the road on your financial journey. It's time to face those challenges head-on and emerge stronger and wiser on the other side.

7.8.1. Why Overcome Financial Obstacles?

Why bother, you might wonder? Because overcoming financial obstacles isn't just about dodging problems—it's about cultivating inner strength and unwavering resolve. It's about transforming setbacks into stepping stones towards a brighter future. Whether it's unexpected expenses, job loss, or economic downturns, facing financial obstacles head-on empowers you to tackle life's twists and turns with grace and resilience.

7.8.2. How to Overcome Financial Obstacles

So, how do you rise above financial challenges when they arise? It begins with facing reality with a clear mind and a courageous heart. Take a deep breath, assess the situation calmly, and explore potential solutions with determination and creativity. Whether it's tightening your belt, exploring new income streams, or seeking guidance from mentors, there's always a way forward.

Take Shirley, for example. When she unexpectedly lost her job during a recession, she was devastated. But instead of letting fear and despair consume her, she sprang into action. She revamped her resume, networked like never before, and even picked up a part-time gig to make ends meet. Finally, her determination paid off, and she landed a new job that not only paid the bills but also aligned more closely with her passions and values.

7.8.3. What to Do: Reflective Questions and Action Steps

Reflective Questions:

1. How do you typically react when faced with financial challenges? Do you tend to panic and feel overwhelmed, or do you approach them with a calm and rational mindset?
2. What lessons have you learned from past financial setbacks, and how have they shaped your approach to handling challenges in the future?
3. In what ways can you utilize your strengths and resources to navigate through present financial hurdles and emerge even more resilient on the other side?

Action Steps:

1. Take stock of the current financial challenge you're facing and break it down into manageable steps.
2. Brainstorm potential solutions and seek input from trusted advisors or friends who have faced similar challenges.
3. Take decisive action to address the problem, whether it's cutting expenses, finding new sources of income, or seeking professional assistance.

Conclusion

In conclusion, overcoming financial obstacles is not just about surviving—it's about thriving in the face of adversity. By accepting challenges as opportunities for growth, learning, and transformation, you can emerge from even the toughest situations with newfound strength and resilience. So, take heart, dear friend, and remember that with courage, perseverance, and determination, you can overcome anything life throws at you.

7.9. Understanding Credit Scores: How to Build and Maintain a Good Credit Score

Hey there! If you're like most folks, you've probably heard the term "credit score" tossed around, but understanding its ins and outs might still feel like a mystery. Don't sweat it! Let's unpack all things credit scores, from what they entail to how they impact your financial landscape.

So, what exactly is a credit score? In plain terms, it's a numerical representation of your creditworthiness—how likely you are to repay loans on time. This score is crafted from a blend of factors, including his credit history, credit utilization, payment track record, types of credit, and length of credit history.

Now, why does having a solid credit score matter? Well, it holds sway over many aspects of your life, from loan approvals to rental applications. Plus, it wields influence over the interest rates slapped onto those loans and credit cards, potentially impacting your wallet in the long haul.

Now, onto the big question: How do you go about bolstering and preserving a commendable credit score? Step one: Kickstart your credit journey by snagging a credit card or snagging a loan. From there, the name of the game is making timely, full payments—late payments can throw a wrench into your score. Plus, it's wise to keep your credit utilization in check, ideally below 30% of your available credit limit. This signals to lenders that you're a responsible credit user who doesn't max out their cards.

And don't forget the importance of keeping tabs on your credit report! You're entitled to a complimentary credit report from each major bureau annually, so be sure to peruse them for any fishy activity or inaccuracies.

In wrapping up, grasping the intricacies of credit scores and mastering the art of building and maintaining a robust one is paramount for your financial health. By establishing credit, staying on top of payments, managing your credit utilization, and routinely reviewing your credit report, you're laying down the groundwork for a solid financial future.

Reflective Questions:

1. What's your current credit score, and how did you acquire that info?
2. Ever missed a payment or gone over your credit limit? If so, how did it affect your credit score?
3. What actions can you take today to boost your credit score?

Action Step: Take a peek at your credit report straightaway and scour it for any hiccups or fraudulent activity. Spot any errors? Waste no time in reaching out to the credit bureau to get things straightened out.

Remember, building and maintaining a stellar credit score is a marathon, not a sprint. But with diligence and responsible credit habits, you're setting yourself up for smooth sailing down the financial road.

7.10. Managing Debt: Strategies for Paying off Debt and Avoiding Debt Traps

Are you struggling with debt and seeking effective strategies to climb out of it while dodging those pesky debt traps? Debt can pack a hefty punch of stress and anxiety but fear not. With the right tactics, you can wrestle back control of your finances and chart a path to freedom. Let's get real and look into some practical ideas for tackling debt and reclaiming your financial sovereignty.

First off, let's get to the root of the issue. What's behind your debt? Overspending? Unexpected expenses? Or perhaps a shortfall in income? Identifying the underlying culprit is key to crafting a plan to tackle your debt head-on.

7.10.1. How to Manage Debt:

- **Identify the Root Causes:** Pinpoint the underlying reasons behind your debt, whether it›s overspending, unexpected expenses, or a shortfall in income. Understanding the root cause of your debt is important for crafting a targeted action plan.
- **Craft a Budget:** Develop a detailed budget that outlines your income and expenses. Track your spending meticulously, differentiate between needs and wants, and cut back on non-essential expenses to free up funds for debt repayment.
- **Consolidate Debt:** Ponder consolidating your loans into a single loan or credit card offering a more favorable interest rate. Such a strategy simplifies your payment process and

reduces the overall interest burden, making it easier to tackle your debt.
- **Avoid Debt Traps:** Steer clear of high-interest credit cards and payday loans, as they can quickly escalate your debt woes. Explore alternative options like low-interest personal loans or balance transfer credit cards to manage your debt more effectively.

7.10.2. What to Do
Action Steps:

1. **Craft a Budget:** One winning strategy? Craft a budget and stick to it like glue. Keep tabs on your spending, discerning between necessities and luxuries, and trim the fat from your expenses. Living within your means frees up precious funds to chip away at that debt pile.
2. **Consolidate Debt:** Explore options for consolidating your debts into a single, lower-interest loan or credit card. This will simplify your payments and reduce the overall interest burden.
3. **Avoid Debt Traps:** Be vigilant and avoid high-interest debt traps that can exacerbate your financial challenges.
4. **Stay Motivated:** Keep your eyes on the prize and stay focused on your debt repayment schedule, celebrating milestones along the way to keep your motivation levels high.

As you embark on your debt-payoff journey, keep your eye on the prize and stay laser-focused on your goals. Sure, it might entail short-term sacrifices, but the payoff—financial freedom—is worth its weight in gold. Remember, the power to reshape your financial destiny lies squarely in your hands.

Reflective Questions:

1. What's driving your debt situation?
2. How can you trim expenses and boost your income?
3. What strategies can you employ to sidestep common debt traps and keep your eyes on the prize?

Action Steps:

1. Craft a budget and monitor your spending.
2. Consolidate your debts into a lower-interest loan or credit card.
3. Steer clear of high-interest debt traps.
4. Stay committed and focused on your financial goals.

In wrapping up, tackling debt demands a proactive mindset and ironclad discipline. By pinpointing the root causes of your debt, crafting a budget, and sidestepping common pitfalls, you're well on your way to seizing control of your financial future. Remember, every step forward counts towards a brighter tomorrow.

7.11. Practicing Gratitude and Generosity with Wealth

7.11.1. Sharing Your Wealth and Being Thankful

Imagine this: You've ascended the rungs of success, standing atop your achievements, surrounded by the rewards of your hard work. Yet amidst the glimmering trophies and accolades, a subtle whisper persists—a gentle reminder that true fulfillment transcends mere wealth; it lies in how we share our abundance and express gratitude along the journey.

Let me illustrate this with a vivid narrative—a tale that echoes the essence of purposeful living. Meet Emma, a woman fueled by ambition and drive, who scaled the peaks of her career. Despite her accomplishments, an emptiness lingered—a longing for deeper significance.

It wasn't until Emma embarked on a quest to give back—volunteering at local shelters and championing causes dear to her heart—that she unearthed the true essence of wealth: the profound joy of impacting lives. Through acts of generosity and gratitude, Emma discovered a richness beyond material possessions—a wealth of purpose and fulfillment.

Dear friends, I implore you to embrace the transformative power of gratitude and generosity with your wealth. Whether through charitable deeds, aiding those in need, or simply acknowledging the abundance in your life, remember that true wealth lies not in accumulation, but in benevolence.

Conclusion

In the grand orchestra of existence, dear readers, let's groove to the beat of purposeful living with hearts flung wide and minds unfettered. In the gospel of "7 Secrets to Purposeful Living: Unlocking Your Path to Happiness and Fulfillment," we've plumbed the depths of discovering and chasing after your cosmic calling.

Keep this close, my friend: Purpose ain't a far-off land to conquer but a groove to vibe with every single day, packed with intent and realness. As you navigate life's crazy maze, may you find solace in the truth that real fulfillment ain't found in fame or validation, but in the sweet melody of connection, growth, and giving back.

So, let's crank up the courage to dream big, question everything, and strut with purpose. Embrace the storms as chances to level up, the setbacks as lessons in courage and grit, and the wins as anthems of your righteous journey.

Now, let's hit that crescendo, live it loud, and rock on with purpose, buddy!

Remember—Discover, Embrace, Flourish, Divine—In rhythm, purpose aligns

Keep rockin' on with purpose, and let's make some magic happen out there!

Fear Not – Trust

AUTHOR BIOGRAPHY

*H*ey lovely readers, I'm thrilled to introduce you to "7 Secrets to Purposeful Living." With over 27 years of experience in media, public relations, coaching, and writing, I've dedicated my career to helping individuals navigate their journey towards success.

In "7 Secrets," I share practical insights and actionable strategies to guide you through your own transformative journey. Drawing from my expertise in communication, leadership, and strategic thinking, I've crafted a clear roadmap for overcoming obstacles, setting meaningful goals, and unlocking your full potential.

As an influencer and thought leader in my field, I'm passionate about sharing real-world examples, personal anecdotes, and proven techniques to inspire you to take action and embark on your path to success.

Hey, are you up for a transformative quest of self-discovery? Let's uncover the secrets to unlocking your full potential and living a deeply meaningful and fulfilling life. Let's get started!

Nita Fleming

EPILOGUE: EMBRACING THE JOURNEY BEYOND

Congratulations, my fellow seekers! Together, we've journeyed through the maze of life's complexities, exploring the depths of purpose and meaning, navigating the twists and turns of relationships, and unlocking the secrets to a purposeful existence. But as we bid adieu to these pages, let us not forget that the journey doesn't end here.

Life, as I'm sure you've gathered by now, is less like a well-marked trail and more like a Choose Your Own Adventure book with missing pages and a broken compass. I remember a time when I was lost in the wilderness, armed only with a map that seemed to lead me in circles. But it was in those moments of uncertainty that I discovered the true beauty of the unknown. And while we've armed ourselves with the insights and revelations from our time together, the real magic happens when we embrace the uncertainty and lean into the discomfort of the unknown.

So, dear friend, as you prepare to move on to the next chapter of your story, remember that You hold the pen, turn the pages, and write the narrative of your life. Embrace the plot twists, relish the character development, and don't be afraid to scribble outside the lines. You are the author of your own adventure.

Therefore, as we bid adieu to these pages, let us treasure the friendships crafted and the memories made. Yo, in the vastness of the unknown, there's a chance to explore, to level up, and to become the heroes of our own epic stories.

So, here's to the uncharted horizons ahead, the adventures yet to be had, and the stories waiting to unfold. Until we meet again, my friends, may your journey be filled with purpose, passion, and a healthy dose of irreverent humor. And remember, it's in the uncertainty that we find our truest selves, so embrace it, lean into it, and let it guide you on your journey.

Stay curious. Stay courageous. And above all, stay true to yourself.

With gratitude,

Nita

AFTERWORD

*H*ey there, awesome readers!

So, here I am, the youngest member of the squad, and they've tasked me with writing this afterword. Pretty cool, right? Well, let's see how it goes!

As I sit down to write this afterword, I can't help but feel a surge of pride and admiration for my mom, the incredible Mother who penned the pages of this book. and let me tell you, it's pretty surreal. Growing up, I watched my Mom pour her heart and soul into crafting this book, and now, holding the finished product in my hands, I can't help but feel a sense of awe. I find myself filled with a mix of emotions—gratitude, nostalgia, and a touch of pride.

This book? It's not just words on paper—it's a roadmap, a guidebook, and a little slice of wisdom all rolled into one. And yeah, okay, maybe I'm biased, but I genuinely believe it's got the power to shake things up, make you think, and maybe even change your life a bit. As I flipped through the pages, I found myself nodding along, recognizing the familiar anecdotes, lessons, and insights that have shaped my own journey.

Now, to everyone who's been on this journey with us, whether you've been here from the start or just stumbled upon us now, I want to say a huge thank you. Your support, your energy, and your vibes have not only kept us going through the highs and lows of this amazing adventure but have also been an integral part of this book's journey. You are the reason this book exists, and for that, we are eternally grateful. I hope you've found something valuable in these pages.

So, as you close the book (literally and metaphorically), I want you to remember something: You're not just a reader; you're the hero of your own story. Yeah, it might sound cheesy, but it's true. This book is just a tool, a guide, but the power to shape your destiny, chase your dreams, and live your best life—it's all within you. All you gotta do is believe in yourself and take that first step. You have the power, and I believe in you.

Alright, that's enough mushy stuff from me. Thanks for hanging out with us, and remember, the world's your playground—so go out there and make some magic happen!

Peace out,

With love and gratitude,

Candy

www.ingramcontent.com/pod-product-compliance
Lightning Source LLC
LaVergne TN
LVHW041927070526
838199LV00051BA/2738